FOOTPATHS OF BRITAIN

NORTH-WEST

p

This is a Parragon Book
First published in 2003

Parragon
Queen Street House
4 Queen Street
Bath BA1 1HE
United Kingdom

Created and produced by
The Bridgewater Book Company Ltd,
Lewes, East Sussex

ISBN: 1-40540-504-X

Printed in China

www.walkingworld.com

Visit the Walkingworld website at
www.walkingworld.com

All the walks in this book are available in more
detailed form on the Walkingworld website.
The route instructions have photographs at
key decision points to help you navigate, and
each walk comes with an Ordnance Survey®
map. Simply print them out on A4 paper
and you are ready to go! A modest annual
subscription gives you access to over 1,400
walks, all in this easy-to-follow format. If you
wish, you can purchase individual walks for a
small fee.

Next to every walk in this book you will see
a Walk ID. You can enter this ID number on
Walkingworld's 'Find a Walk' page and you will
be taken straight to the details of that walk.

CONTENTS

Introduction

Britain is a fabulous place to walk. We are blessed with a varied and beautiful landscape, a dense network of public footpaths and places of historical interest at every corner. Add to all this the many thousands of well-placed pubs, tea shops and visitor attractions, and it's easy to see why walking is a treasured pastime for millions of people.

Walking is the perfect way to keep fit and healthy. It is good for your heart, muscles and body generally, without making the extreme demands of many sports. For most walkers, however, the health benefits are secondary. We walk for the sheer pleasure of it — being able to breathe in the fresh air, enjoy the company of our friends and 'get away from it all'.

Equipment

If you take up walking as a hobby, it is quite possible to spend a fortune on specialist outdoor kit. But you really don't need to. Just invest in a few inexpensive basics and you'll be ready to enjoy any of the walks in this book.

For footwear, boots are definitely best as they provide you with ankle support and protection from the inevitable mud, nettles and puddles. A lightweight pair should be fine if you have no intention of venturing up big hills or over rugged terrain. If you are not sure what to get, go to a specialist shop and ask for advice. Above all, choose boots that fit well and are comfortable.

Take clothing to deal with any weather that you may encounter. Allow for the 'wind-chill' factor – if your clothes get wet you will feel this cooling effect even more. Carry a small rucksack with a spare top, a hat and waterproofs, just in case. The key is being able to put on and take off layers of clothing at will and so keep an even, comfortable temperature throughout the day.

It's a good idea to carry some food and drink. Walking is exercise and you need to replace the fluid you lose through perspiration. Take a bottle of soft drink or water, and sip it regularly rather than downing it in one go. The occasional chocolate bar, sandwich or biscuit can work wonders when energy levels are flagging.

Walking poles – the modern version of the walking stick – are worth considering. They help you to balance and allow your arms to take some of the strain when going uphill. They also lessen the impact on your knees on downhill slopes. Don't be fooled into thinking that poles are just for the older walker – they are popular with trekkers and mountaineers of all ages.

Finding your way

Most walkers use Ordnance Survey® maps, rightly considered to be among the most accurate, up-to-date and 'walker-friendly' in the world. The 1:50,000 scale Landranger series has long been a favourite of outdoor enthusiasts. Almost all areas of Britain are also covered by the more detailed 1:25,000 scale Explorer and Explorer OL series. These include features such as field boundaries, farm buildings and small streams.

Having a map and compass – and learning how to use them – is vital to being safe in the countryside. Compass and map skills come with practice – there is no substitute for taking them out and having a go. Buy a compass with a transparent base plate and rotating dial; you will find this type in any outdoor shop. Most come with simple instructions – if not, ask in the shop for a guide.

If this all sounds a bit serious, I urge you not to worry too much about getting lost. We have all done it – some of us more often than we care to admit! You are unlikely to come to much harm unless you are on a featureless hilltop or out in very poor weather. If you want to build up your confidence, start with shorter routes through farmland or along the coastline and allow yourself plenty of time.

There are plenty of walks in this book that are perfect for the beginner. You can make navigating even easier by downloading the routes in this book from Walkingworld's website: www.walkingworld.com. These detailed walk instructions feature a photograph at each major decision point, to help you confirm your position and see where to go next.

Another alternative is to join a local walking group

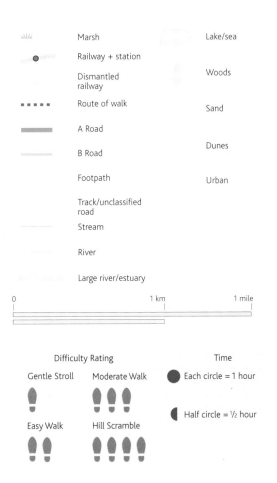

Marsh		Lake/sea
Railway + station		
Dismantled railway		Woods
Route of walk		
A Road		Sand
B Road		Dunes
Footpath		Urban
Track/unclassified road		
Stream		
River		
Large river/estuary		

0   1 km   1 mile

Difficulty Rating

Gentle Stroll   Moderate Walk

Easy Walk   Hill Scramble

Time

Each circle = 1 hour

Half circle = ½ hour

and learn from others. There are hundreds of such groups around the country, with members keen to share their experience and skills.

Enough words. Take the walks in this book as your inspiration. Grab your map and compass, and put on your boots. It's time to go out and walk!

Have fun.

DAVID STEWART *Walkingworld*

▲ Map: Explorer 255 or 256
▲ Distance: 10.6 km/6½ miles
▲ Walk ID: 312 Jim Grindle

Difficulty rating

Time

▲ Hills or Fells, River, Pub, Toilets, Museum, Castle, Stately Home, Birds, Flowers, Great Views

Llangollen Canal Walk

A walk along the canal with a return by bridleway, which snakes round the hillside offering outstanding views. The walk includes a climb to the top of Dinas Bran, the ancient castle overlooking the town of LLangollen.

1 Turn right from the car park entrance and walk to the main street. Turn left. Cross the bridge and go half-left across the main road to a passageway with a signpost for canal boats. Go up the narrow path or steps. On the towpath turn right and go under the road bridge. Follow the towpath for 2 km to reach another bridge.

2 Cross the stile by the gate and turn left on the lane, crossing the canal bridge. Go uphill until you reach Llandyn Hall. On the left is a stile. Go over and up to another stile by a gate 200 m away. Cross the two stiles near to each other. Go half-left across the field. Go through the gate and follow the hedge and then the buildings on the left until you reach a stile onto a lane. Turn right. You will reach a kissing gate and signpost for the castle.

3 Follow the signpost pointing left. Go over the stile at the end of the path and turn left. Go straight uphill to the castle. On the far side you will be able to pick up a broad, fenced track leading down. Turn right at the second tree. Continue until you reach a fence. Turn left and go down towards a stile. Cross the field to the far right corner to a stile by a lane.

4 Turn right and stay on the lane for 500 m. Turn right at the junction and look for the signpost for Brynhyfryd.

Turn left and pass a building close on your left and two others up to the right. Go through a gate and onto a grassy track for 1.2 km after which it drops and joins another. Turn left so that you double back. In 120 m you come to a ladder stile on the right. Cross and look for another one in the corner. Go over and follow the field edge.

5 Follow the sign towards Llangollen. You soon come to a gate. Follow an enclosed track to a road. Turn right. You come to a canal bridge on the left.

6 Cross the bridge, turn left and follow the towpath for 2 km back to Llangollen.

access information

Llangollen is just off the A5 and is signposted from the A483. There is a car park in the centre of town, again well signposted. There are regular buses to Chester, Chirk, Wrexham and Oswestry.

The Offa's Dyke path, which runs along the hills above Llangollen, traces the border built between England and Wales in 770, when Wales effectively became a separate Celtic nation.

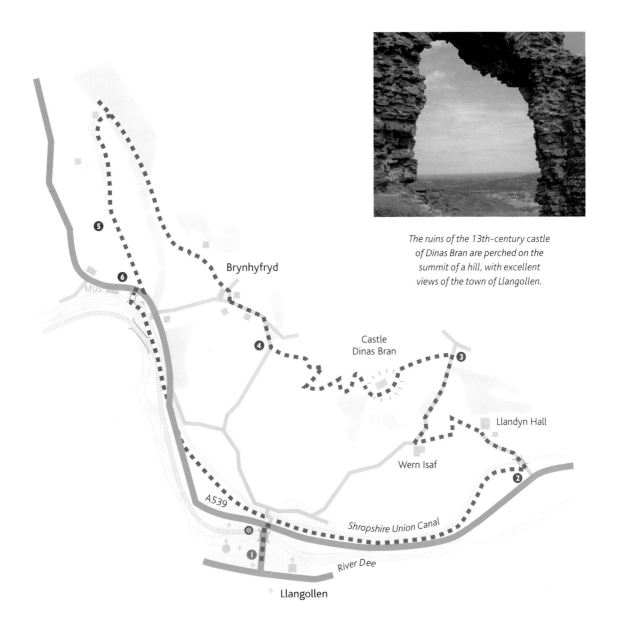

The ruins of the 13th-century castle of Dinas Bran are perched on the summit of a hill, with excellent views of the town of Llangollen.

Brynhyfryd

Mus

Castle
Dinas Bran

Llandyn Hall

Wern Isaf

A539

Shropshire Union Canal

River Dee

Llangollen

0   1 km   1 mile

▲ Map: Explorer 256 & 257
▲ Distance: 10 km/6¼ miles
▲ Walk ID: 139 Jim Grindle

Difficulty rating

Time

▲ River, Pub, Toilets, Wildlife, Flowers, Great Views

Erbistock from Overton

The 'Overton Yew Trees' walk follows the River Dee. The route then climbs and the views are spectacular. A further riverside walk is followed by a second climb to the village.

1 Go through the gate into the churchyard at Overton, with its famous 12th-century yew trees. Cross the road and turn left, passing the war memorial, and walk as far as the sharp bend left.

2 Turn right at the signpost for Maelor Way. Follow the road down the hill to where it curves right. The track goes into the field and makes a dog-leg onto the embankment. Follow this track to the river bank.

3 Turn left at a signpost and keep to the right of the field. The River Dee runs just behind the trees. A footbridge leads to a narrow path through the woods parallel to the river. Leave by another bridge and a stile into a small field. Keep to the right edge and make for the corner. Cross the stile and continue until you are opposite an inn on the far bank of the river.

4 Turn left, up the embankment, via some steps to a stile at the top. Turn left at the stile and then right to follow the line of some fencing uphill to another stile. This stile leads to some steps. Turn left and soon you will cross a stile by a cattle grid. Cross another stile on the left further on into a field. Follow the line of the hedge on the left to a signpost. This directs you half-right round two lines of trees. You must come back left again to a stile almost in the bottom left corner of the field.

5 Beyond the next stile is a path

The River Dee, with its rocky bed, swirls and eddies, and tree-lined banks, flows through peaceful villages and areas of unspoilt natural beauty.

access information

Overton is most easily reached from the A483 (Wrexham bypass). Turn onto the A539 (signposted Ruabon and then Erbistock). Continue on the A539 at the junction with the A528. There is a car park at the back of the church. The main street is wide and has ample parking.

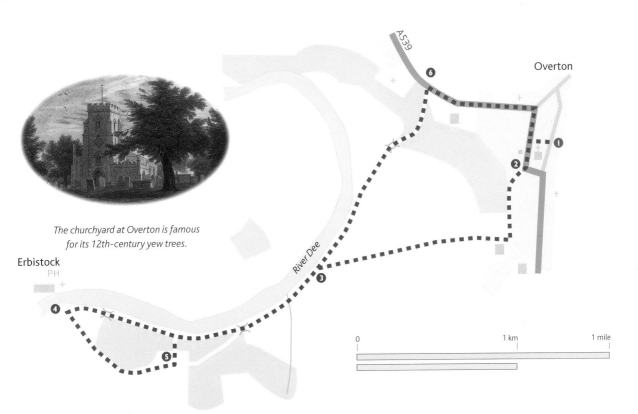

The churchyard at Overton is famous for its 12th-century yew trees.

Overton

A539

Erbistock

PH

River Dee

0   1 km   1 mile

leading back to the riverside path. Turn right and follow your outward route. At the point where you joined the river, continue alongside the river on the left of the field until you come to a wire fence and a stile. Cross and turn right. Follow the line of the fence as it turns left and then sharp right. Look out ahead of you for a signpost by a gate and a bridge. The path beyond the bridge curves left and uphill. The path ends at the main road, the A539.

6 Cross to the pavement on the far side of the road and turn right for the centre of Overton, back to your starting point.

▲ Map: Explorer 256
▲ Distance: 6.5 km/4 miles
▲ Walk ID: 226 Jim Grindle

Difficulty rating

Time

▲ River, Sculpture Trail, Ancient Monument, Woodland

Alyn Waters from Gresford Bells

The walk begins and ends in Alyn Waters Country Park near Gresford Bells. The park has been created from the site of a large opencast mine and has a sculpture trail. Gradually it moves into tranquil fields by the River Alyn.

❶ From the gate at the lower end of the car park follow the path until you reach a silver sculpture. Take the right fork. When you reach a gateway on a lane, turn left. You will see a fork in the road. Take the right fork, downhill. The lane crosses the River Alyn and climbs again.

❷ At a sharp left bend go through the kissing gate on the right. Follow the path until you come to a junction with a path. Turn left and follow the path to a gateway. Turn left and go through a car park to the main road. At the road, turn right and continue until you reach the football ground.

❸ Go in, keeping near an embankment on the left. Turn left into a gap in the trees and pick up a little path leading down to Sherbourne Avenue. Turn right and in 120 m cross to a signpost. The path passes along the backs of houses to a kissing gate. Go through and turn left. Just after passing the pond on the left the fence takes a sharp turn to the left. Pass a gate with no fence round it to reach a broader track. Turn right here and in 50 m you come to a solitary tree. Turn left by the tree and pick up a path that follows the stream to a kissing gate and a main road. Cross the road to the path on the far side.

❹ Turn right into the lane. It goes sharp left after only 20 m to a group of farm buildings. Go between all the buildings

Majestic beech trees and deciduous woodland border the River Alyn, part of the Alyn Waters Country Park.

to the bottom gate. Cross the metal stile and go towards a ruined building. Cross the footbridge over the River Alyn and turn right and follow the river. The route leads past two gates and stiles to a small lane by some houses. Continue to reach a T-junction.

❺ Turn left and follow the lane to a crossroads with the B5425. Cross to the lane opposite (Park Road) and walk as far as a sharp left bend, where there is a stile.

❻ Cross the stile into Alyn Waters Country Park. There is a narrow green path that you should follow. Cross the broader green path and continue until you come to a tarmac path. Turn right and you will see the car park.

further information

There has been a remarkable transformation of what was once a huge mining area. The latest development, and one which has added an interesting twist to the area, is the creation of a sculpture trail. A few of these witty and entertaining sculptures are passed on this walk, but a wheelchair user could stay in the park and track down many more.

access information

The start of the walk is in the car park of
a public golf driving range less than 4 km
north-west of Gresford. It is on the west
side of the B5425. There are buses from the
centre of Wrexham.

Alyn Waters
Country Park

Bryn Alyn

Gwersyllt

B5425

0   1 km   1 mile

▲ Map: Explorer OL 17
▲ Distance: 8 km/5 miles
▲ Walk ID: 1419 Jim Grindle

Difficulty rating

Time

▲ Hills or Fells, Mountains, River, Toilets, National Trust/NTS, Birds, Food Shop, Tea Shop

Ogwen from Bethesda

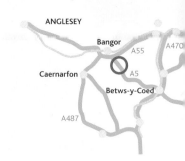

From Bethesda the walk descends into the valley and then offers an easy climb up to Ogwen Cottage and Ogwen Falls. An unusual landmark to look out for is a quartz stone by the side of the track.

The rugged, glaciated peaks of Snowdonia form a dramatic backdrop to this walk.

1 Start in the town centre and follow the A5 south. You will go over a river bridge and come to a crossroads on the edge of town. Turn left at the Snowdonia National Park emblem, then right into a street called Rhes James. Go through a gate at the end of this short street.
2 Follow the track and go through another gate. Follow the grass verge through to the woods. The path ends at a stile leading onto open ground. You will find a grassy track that soon turns sharply left. Follow the path. When it fades out, turn right near the remains of a sheepfold into a shallow valley. Make your way up the slope.

further information

A few minutes from the end of this walk is Cwm Idwal, a National Nature Reserve noted for its geomorphology and geology as well as for its rare Arctic-alpine plants.

3 Follow the higher ground until you see a wall on the right and then follow faint tracks alongside it. One kilometre from here you will cross the first of three streams and go through a gate in the wall leading you into the sheepfold. On the far side of the sheepfold is a stile by a gate – and a yellow arrow.
4 Cross the stile and turn left – there is another signpost on the far side of the wall. Follow the wall to another gate and stile about 100 m away. When you are over this stile look for posts with yellow arrows. They guide you onto a grassy track that leads gently downhill. After 1.5 km watch out for trees surrounding buildings below you on the right. By the track is a quartz stone.
5 The main track continues down to the A5. The right of way doubles back at the quartz stone to a gate in the corner. Go through the gate and follow paths down to the A5. Cross to a fingerpost. Go through onto a path leading to a bridge. The path goes over the bridge, left alongside the low wall and then passes a huge glaciated boulder and a smaller bridge to reach the old road.
6 Turn left and after a climb and 2.5 km you will reach the Youth Hostel at Ogwen. On the main road is Ogwen Cottage and the bus stop.

Accessible in any weather, this walk offers outstanding views of a number of Wales' 3,000 peaks.

access information

Bethesda is on the A5 south-east of Bangor.
Buses run from Betws-y-Coed to Bethesda
and Bangor. There are several signposted car
parks in the town. At the end of the walk you
have several choices. You can walk back to
Bethesda or wait for a bus if you are not
being collected here.

▲ Map: Explorer OL 17
▲ Distance: 4.5 km/2¾ miles
▲ Walk ID: 757 Peter Salenieks

Difficulty rating

Time

▲ Mountains, Lake/Loch, Toilets, Great Views

Twll Du (Devil's Kitchen) from Ogwen Cottage

A historic view of the falls at Twll Du (Devil's Kitchen).

A short, scenic circuit of Llyn Idwal from Ogwen Cottage, with views up into Twll Du and across to Pen yr Ole Wen. Ogwen Valley is worth a visit for its splendid glaciated landforms.

❶ The walk starts at the eastern end of the car park. Follow the stone path south, crossing a double stile and then a wooden footbridge. The path bends round to the left, before swinging back to the right after about 200 m. Follow the path to Llyn Idwal, go through a gate and continue along the eastern side of the lake. After passing Idwal Slabs, the path climbs towards the stream.

❷ Cross the stream and continue more steeply along the path until you reach a path junction beside a large boulder.

❸ For a better view into Twll Du, turn left at the large boulder and ascend a little further. When you have finished, continue along the path in front of the large boulder. Turn north and descend towards Llyn Idwal. Stone slabs bridge several small streams as the path goes along the western side of the lake. Bear right along the northern edge of Llyn Idwal, joining the path from Y Garn just before you reach a wooden footbridge.

❹ Cross the footbridge and turn left at the footpath junction, finally rejoining your outward route back to the car park at Ogwen Cottage.

further information

This walk will take about 90 minutes. While it should present few difficulties in good conditions, this is graded as a moderate walk because the stream crossing can be awkward. Under winter conditions, the upper section is deceptively icy and should only be attempted by suitably experienced and equipped parties.

access information

Cars can be parked in the pay-and-display car park at Ogwen Cottage. This is approached from the A5(T), either travelling west from Capel Curig or east from Bethesda. If this car park is full, there are lay-bys beside Llyn Ogwen, a few hundred metres east along the A5(T). There is also a bus service to Ogwen.

ANGLESEY
Conwy
Bangor
A55
Caernarfon
Betws-y-Coed
A487
A470

Ogwen Cottage
PC
A5(T)

Llyn Idwal

National Nature Reserve

Twll Du (Devil's Kitchen)

0   1 km   1 mile

▲ Map: Explorer OL 23
▲ Distance: 8 km/5 miles
▲ Walk ID: 604 Chris Dixon

Difficulty rating

Time

▲ Mountains, River, Pub, Birds, Good for Wheelchairs

Mawddach Estuary from Penmaenpool

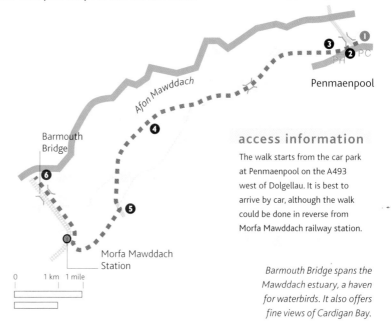

Following the route of a dismantled railway towards the sea, this walk takes in splendid views of the hilly countryside. The estuary at Barmouth Bridge is a haven for waders and other waterbirds. Parts of the walk pass unspoilt ancient woodland.

1 At the car park you will see a hut and the toll-bridge behind it at the start of the walk. From here, head downstream without crossing the river.

2 Just over a small road is a hotel, converted from the old Penmaenpool railway station. The remainder of this walk is along the course of the old railway as it heads towards the sea.

3 Pass through the gate, and after a slight bend the path heads for a kilometre straight across the marsh before reaching the estuary itself. After a further kilometre, you will cross a footbridge.

4 About 2 km later, you may start to get views of the distant Barmouth Bridge.

5 You can choose to take the road leading to Morfa Mawddach Station (formerly Barmouth Junction), or follow the route down the track on the right and past a disused platform. If you go to the station, a gate at the end of the one remaining platform links back up with the route.

6 Barmouth Bridge can be crossed for a small toll, but since the toll booth is at the far side, you can easily go half way for a view out to sea or back up the estuary. From here, retrace your steps to Penmaenpool.

access information

The walk starts from the car park at Penmaenpool on the A493 west of Dolgellau. It is best to arrive by car, although the walk could be done in reverse from Morfa Mawddach railway station.

Barmouth Bridge spans the Mawddach estuary, a haven for waterbirds. It also offers fine views of Cardigan Bay.

▲ Map: Explorer 262

▲ Distance: 10 km/6¼ miles

▲ Walk ID: 635 Chris Dixon

Difficulty rating

Time

▲ Sea, Toilets, Church, National Trust/NTS, Wildlife, Birds, Great Views

Ynys y Fydlyn from Porth Swtan

This walk begins on the cliffs on Anglesey's north-west coast. After a view of the island of Ynys y Fydlyn the walk heads inland and there is an option to take in one of Anglesey's best viewpoints.

❶ Leave the car park, and head towards the sea. Go through the gate, along the headland. When you reach a junction bear left and keep to the coast. When you reach a stile to the right, cross over it and continue. After a kilometre or so you climb up to a cairn.

❷ From here, dropping down a fairly steep slope, you will reach a bridge. Cross the bridge and take the lesser of two paths, keeping to the left and to the cliffs.

❸ Upon rounding the headland called Trwyn y Cerwyn there is a view of the island, Ynys y Fydlyn. From the beach, looking east, you will see a small marshy lake, and a track climbing to its right. Take the track and keep to the side of the forest. You soon join a track which leads to the road.

❹ When you reach the road, turn left and after about 200 m, you should turn right onto a track to Hen-dy farmhouse. Continue through the gate. Follow the path round the pond in the marshy area ahead, and head for the white gate on the horizon, which will let you into

another farm. Go round the back of the building on the left, through another gate, and then up to the far corner of the field, where it meets the road. Turn right along the road.

❺ After about 300 metres, take the path to the left. Head to the left of Myndd y Garn, then turn right across the bottom of the peak. Continue along the path back to the road, and turn left. After a few minutes walking, another road joins from the right. At the next fork turn right and continue on the road to the church.

❻ Follow the road back to Porth Swtan, and turn right to return to the car park.

A lighthouse perches on the barren island of Holyhead, which lies to the north-west of Anglesey, and is connected to it by a rocky causeway.

further information

The island of Ynys y Fydlyn is easily accessible except at high tide. There is a small beach and a large cave.

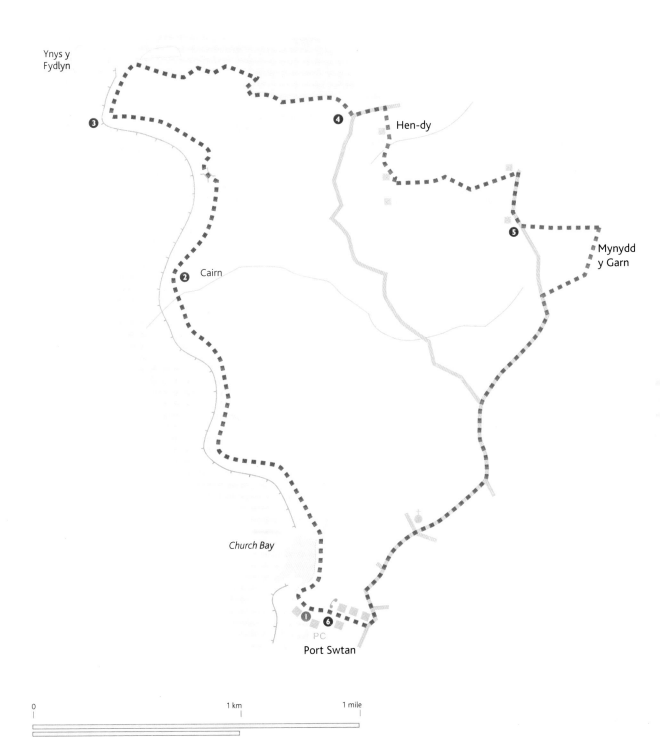

Ynys y
Fydlyn

3

Hen-dy

4

5

Mynydd
y Garn

Cairn

2

Church Bay

1
PC

6

Port Swtan

0

1 km

1 mile

▲ Map: Explorer 264
▲ Distance: 22 km/13¾ miles
▲ Walk ID: 753 Jim Grindle

Difficulty rating

Time

▲ Sea, Pub, Toilets, Church, Great Views

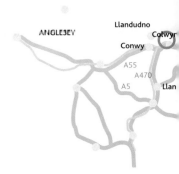

Rhyl from Rhôs-on-Sea (Colwyn Bay)

This is an easy-to-follow linear walk along the coast, using a specially made path as well as promenades and sea walls. It goes from west to east to take advantage of the prevailing wind.

Bodnant Castle boasts one of the finest gardens in Britain, famous for its display of rhododendrons, azaleas and magnolias. Perched above the River Conwy valley, the gardens offer fine views of Snowdonia.

❶ Keep Rhôs-on-Sea Information Centre building on your left to begin the walk. After 2 km you approach Colwyn Bay Pier. After another 2 km you have passed Old Colwyn, and the promenade now turns under the railway. A tarmac path branches off on the left. Follow this path.

❷ In 1 km the path rises by sea defence blocks. After another 3 km you cross a bridge. Keep going now for 5 km.

❸ Once you reach the front at Pensarn the railway station of Pensarn and Abergele is only 500 m further on, should you wish to return to Colwyn Bay. The footpath continues between the wall and the railway.

❹ Head towards Rhyl where there is a group of small buildings. Go through the metal kissing gate and onto a red shale path which winds through the dunes. About 300 m away there is a junction with a tarmac path.

❺ Turn right and go through a gate just in front of the bungalows. Go a little to the right to keep in the same direction down Betws Avenue. Turn to the left into Bryn Avenue. At the end of the road turn right and you will reach the Ferry Inn. The main road is just in front. Turn left and make for the bridge over the River Clwyd. Across the river there is a roundabout. Go straight over, following the sign to the railway station, which is still 2 km away. You can walk alongside the Marine Lake for a little. Keep going until you come to the traffic lights by the police station. The railway station is signposted again from here.

❻ From Rhyl you can return to Colwyn Bay by train or taxi.

access information

By car use the A55 Expressway, turning off at the signs for Llandudno and Rhôs-on-Sea. Turn right at the first two sets of traffic lights and right at the first roundabout. Go straight over the next roundabout and turn right at the next lights. This is Rhôs Road which leads directly to a T-junction by the Information Centre.

Views across Colwyn Bay make this a footpath to remember.

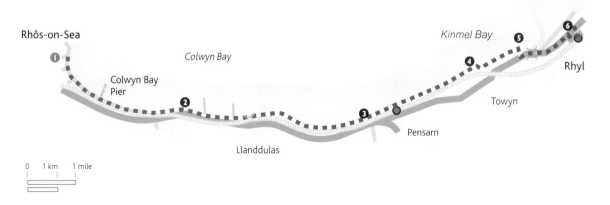

Rhôs-on-Sea

1

Colwyn Bay

Colwyn Bay
Kinmel Bay

Colwyn Bay
Pier

2

3

Pensarn

Llanddulas

4

Towyn

5

6

Rhyl

0   1 km   1 mile

▲ Map: Explorer 275
▲ Distance: 8 km/5 miles
▲ Walk ID: 256 Ian Darbyshire

Difficulty rating

Time

▲ River, Lake/Loch, Sea, Pub, Toilets, National Trust/NTS, Wildlife, Birds, Flowers, Great Views, Good for Wheelchairs

Hightown from Waterloo

This linear walk explores the seashore and sandhills that stretch between Waterloo Station, in the northern suburbs of Liverpool, and the Alt estuary near Hightown. It is a rewarding route for bird-watching enthusiasts.

❶ Turn left from Waterloo Station and walk down South Road to the distant promenade, past the Marine Gardens. Follow the path to the right of Sefton Coastal Park. Go between the two lakes to reach the beach side of the promenade. Carry on up the path towards the promenade. Turn right and follow the promenade, either along the path or along the beach.

❷ Keep going until you reach the coastguard station at Hall Road. The stone wall at the end of the promenade is a favourite place for fishermen at high tide. If you wish you can cut the walk short here and walk inland along Hall Road West to Hall Road Station, about half a kilometre away. Alternatively you can take the little path from the car park.

❸ To continue, remain with the shore beyond the end of the promenade, going along the path. Between the two beached lightships is a good place to look for wading birds such as oystercatchers, redshank and dunlin.

❹ Just past the second lightship bear right at the waymark along a path through the low sandhills. This winds through growths of creeping willow, tough grasses and stands of sea buckthorn. Turn left where the path forks by a post. Follow the white-topped posts to reach the sailing clubhouse. Here a board points the way to a viewpoint (at low tide) over the remains of an ancient submerged forest.

❺ Rejoin the path through the dunes. Follow the white-topped posts leading to the Alt estuary and a boatyard. Keep an eye out for shore birds including the curlew and the bar-tailed godwit in the Alt estuary.

❻ Walk up the path to the road and turn right. Go down the road, cross the roundabout and keep ahead along Lower Alt Road to find Hightown Station.

access information

Take a train to Waterloo Mersey Station. The suggested return is from Hall Road Station for a short walk, or Hightown Station for the longer walk – trains run every 15 minutes.

Liverpool's revitalized 19th-century dockside area now includes shops, restaurants, art galleries and commercial premises.

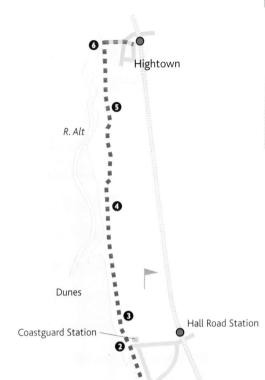

6
Hightown

5

R. Alt

4

Dunes

3
Coastguard Station

2

Hall Road Station

Blundellsands

Waterloo

Marine
Lake

further information

Waterloo to Hall Road is accessible to
wheelchair users. For a longer challenge the
Sefton Coastal Path links the entire length
from Waterloo to Southport, crossing high
sandhills and meandering through shady
pine woods and rich farmland. It is
waymarked throughout by yellow disks with
a toad on them. Linking paths lead to all the
stations on the Northern Line.

0   1 km   1 mile

▲ Map: Explorer 285
▲ Distance: 6 km/3¾ miles
▲ Walk ID: 257 Jim Grindle

Difficulty rating

Time

▲ Sea, Pub, Toilets, National Trust/NTS, Wildlife, Birds, Flowers, Great Views, Good for Wheelchairs

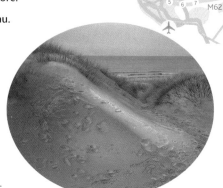

Fisherman's Path from Freshfield

This walk follows the railway line and enters pine woods before reaching the shore. Views from the beach take in the North Wales Clwydian Hills and the Carneddau. In clear conditions you can see the Lake District.

❶ On leaving the station turn left and left again at the telephone box. Walk past a row of shops and then the station car park. At the end of the car park continue on the road which becomes a gravelled track. Take the wide left fork following the railway line as far as the level crossing.

❷ Go over the railway line and follow the track through a golf course until you reach a metal gate at the entrance to the National Nature Reserve.

❸ Take the left fork, which takes you for 1 km between the golf course on the left and the Reserve on the right. Go through a more open area and you reach a junction by the sand dunes.

❹ Take the fork left, which has woods to the left and the sea behind the dunes to the right. After 1 km the path leads to the beach. Walk along the beach. The paths going off the beach are marked by posts. Continue as far as the fourth post, marked Victoria Road South, then turn left and climb by the fence to the top of the dunes.

❺ A boardwalk leads down into the car park. Keep going until you reach a road leading to the Wardens' hut. Look on the right for 'Squirrel Walk' – this is the best place to see red squirrels.

❻ Keep straight on and the concrete road gives way to tarmac – Victoria Road. It is now less than 1 km back to the station directly down this road.

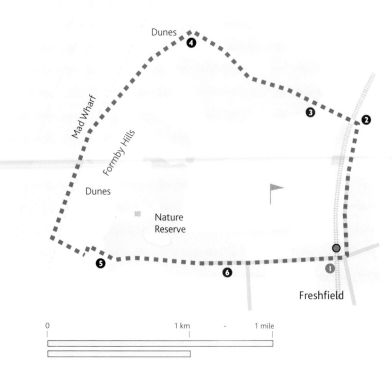

The hills of North Wales can be viewed from the sand dunes of Formby Point.

access information

The walk starts at Freshfield Station on the Southport/Liverpool line. Access by road is from the A565. Follow the tourist signs to Formby Point (National Trust). The route crosses the railway line where there is parking.

▲ Map: Explorer 286
▲ Distance: 14.5 km/9 miles
▲ Walk ID: 732 Jim Grindle

Difficulty rating

Time

▲ Sea, Pub, Toilets, Play Area, Birds,
Great Views, Good for Wheelchairs

Blackpool from Fleetwood

This is a linear walk along the Lancashire coast, from Fleetwood to the Pleasure Beach in Blackpool. By keeping to the beach where possible, and using the lower levels of the walks along the sea defences, you can keep well away from traffic.

❶ Cross the road from the North Euston Hotel and turn left on the promenade until you reach the pier 200 m away. Continue for another 50 m past the pier until you come to a turning on the right, beside a noticeboard, which brings you to the sea wall. Keeping to the beach or the embankment, turn and follow the promenade as it curves to the left. Simply continue south, with the sea to your right, until you reach Cleveleys.
❷ Continue on the promenade until the path curves up to the left to meet the main road. Continue to head south along the road.
❸ At Little Bispham you can turn left if you prefer to catch a tram back to Fleetwood, or you can carry on south to Blackpool (you may have to walk

access information

You can take a train to Blackpool and then a tram to the terminus in Fleetwood. By road it is easiest to come by the M6 to junction 32; the M55 to junction 3 and then the A585 to Fleetwood. There is free parking near the North Euston Hotel which is right on the sea front at the very north of Fleetwood.

along the upper promenade for part of the way if restoration work is taking place). Carry straight on along the promenade until you reach Blackpool's North Pier.
❹ If you wish to extend the walk, it is 3.5 km from here, past the South Pier, to the Pleasure Beach at Blackpool. You can then take a tram back to Fleetwood.

Blackpool's piers offer a delightful mix of nostalgia and scenic beauty for those walkers happy to continue to the end of this route.

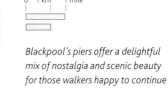

▲ Map: Explorer OL 7
▲ Distance: 11 km/6¾ miles
▲ Walk ID: 919 William Kembery

Difficulty rating

👣👣👣

Time

●●●

River, Sea, Pub, Toilets, National
Trust/NTS, Wildlife, Birds, Flowers,
Great Views, Food Shop, Good for Kids,
Moor, Tea Shop, Woodland

Leighton Moss and Jenny Brown's Point

This is a varied walk through woods and along quiet lanes. The walk includes
a stretch of Morecambe Bay's rich shores.

❶ From the car park take the little gate into Eave's Wood. At the first T-junction turn left. Soon take the right-hand fork going uphill through the trees. At the next junction keep straight on, swinging slightly left.

❷ Turn left off the track, but do not go through the gate. Turn right with a stone wall on the left and a hedge on the right. You will arrive at a lane by a bench and a signpost pointing right to Arnside Tower. Cross straight over, along a little lane opposite signed to Cove Road. Follow the narrow lane when it divides, towards a little gate to the left of a house.

❸ Go through the gate and on to the lane. Go straight on, to pick up the footpath again. Above Cove Road turn right and, when the footpath ends, cross the road and take the footpath on the other side. As it swings right, take the little road off to the left, signposted to the shore. Go through the gate and turn left along the shore, keeping near the base of the cliffs.

❹ After about 1 km, take a little road leading up from the shore. Go through the gate stile to follow the road. Soon take a right-hand footpath, signposted Lindeth Road. At the road, turn right and follow it until it forks with Hollins Lane going off to the left.

❺ Take the right-hand fork signed Jenny Brown's Point. Look out for a little gate on the right. Go through the gate and follow the good footpath across the heathland round to the left, parallel to the wall. Follow the footpath down into the bay. Continue with the footpath through the trees. Soon pass through two kissing gates. Turn right along the road. Just before Jenny Brown's Houses take the little causeway down on to the shore and past the old smelt chimney. Follow the base of the cliffs to a stile.

❻ Go through and continue with the fence on the right. At a metal gate go straight on. The footpath slopes gently uphill into the woods from a solid stone stile. At the road turn right and at the first junction turn right again. At the next major junction keep straight on towards the station. Soon a little lane goes off to the left. Take this lane to return to the car park.

access information

Silverdale is west of the M6,
north of Morecambe Park. Begin
the walk at Eave's Wood car park,
north of Silverdale train station.
If arriving by public transport,
there is a regular train service
from Lancaster or Carlisle.

The extensive tidal flats of Morecambe Bay are one of the most important bird reserves in Britain.

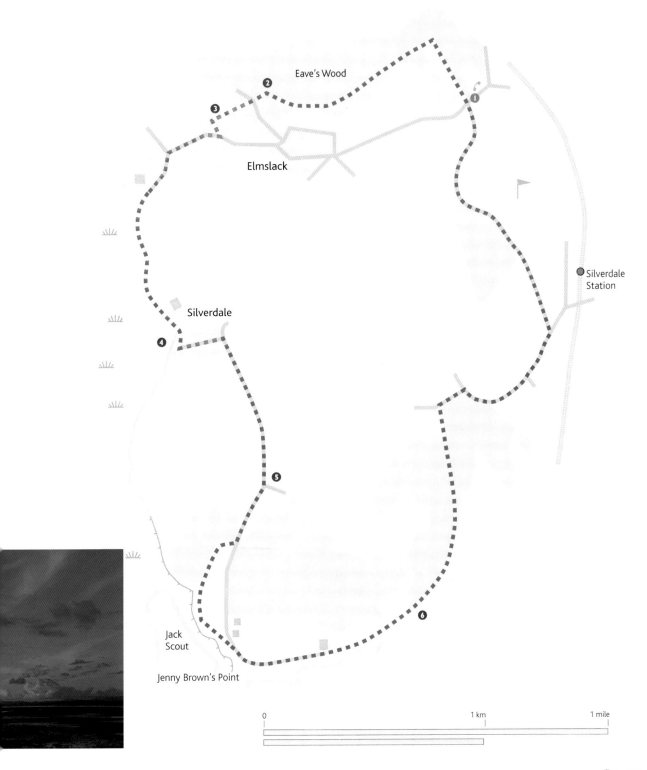

Eave's Wood

2

3

Elmslack

Silverdale

1

Silverdale
Station

4

5

6

Jack
Scout

Jenny Brown's Point

0   1 km   1 mile

▲ Map: Explorer OL 7
▲ Distance: 14 km/8¾ miles
▲ Walk ID: 657 William Kembery

Difficulty rating

Time

▲ Hills or Fells, River, Pub, Toilets, Museum, Church, Birds, Flowers

Ulverston Sands and Birkrigg Common

A very scenic walk that takes in the Birkrigg Stone Circle and Conishead, a Buddhist priory. In the summer you can visit this retreat, but at other times stay on the track along the shoreline.

1 From the car park walk up the quiet lane and turn right at the top into Bardsea. Take the first road on the left. At the bottom of the hill, swing left towards Wellhouse and walk through the hamlet. Follow the road/track up the hill, now heading for Birkrigg Common. Continue until almost at a little unfenced road. Turn right and walk over the small rise.

2 Follow the stone wall, then the green track up the hillside. At the brow of the hill, curve around to the right to find the white trig point. From here head directly north towards the Hoad Memorial. Go back down on one of the grassy tracks. Follow the signpost to Far Mount Barrow and head for a gate left of the corner of a wall. This leads on to an enclosed lane, which you should follow. Turn right and then first left on to a farm track.

3 Go through the gate into the farmyard and pass to the right of the barn on a road and join the farm. Turn right at the Priory Road signpost and walk along the good track. Go through an iron kissing gate and continue between the hedges. Stay with the right-hand hedge to another iron kissing gate to join a track.

4 Soon you go through another kissing gate on the left. Keep the wall on the right. Left of a small wood go through another kissing gate. Head just left of the farmhouse to yet another kissing gate and join the farm lane down to the road. Turn right and 100 m down the road, turn left through a gap stile. Follow the right-hand fence as it turns right, over a ladder stile, then left until it emerges on to the road over another stile. Turn left along the lane and take a stile by the first gate on the right. Follow a faint track across the field to two stiles crossing a ditch.

5 Head half-left to the left of a row of houses, climb a stile by a gate and walk down the back road of the houses to a lane and turn left. At the T-junction at Sandhall turn left and in about 20 m go through a kissing gate on the right.

6 Almost doubling back, head for the left of a wood towards a gate. Through the gate walk with the trees on the right along a rough track and eventually via two further gates join a lane. Follow this round to the shore. Turn right on the track and walk along the shoreline past Conishead Priory. The path leads eventually back to the car park near Bardsea where you began.

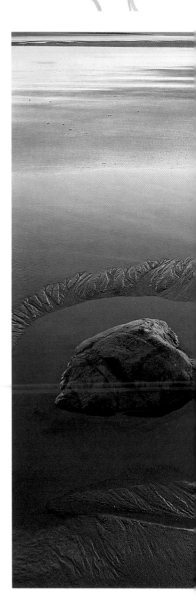

Walking across Ulverston Sands at sunrise or sunset, the shore can be bathed in wonderful colours. As with all coastal walks, you should check the tides before setting out.

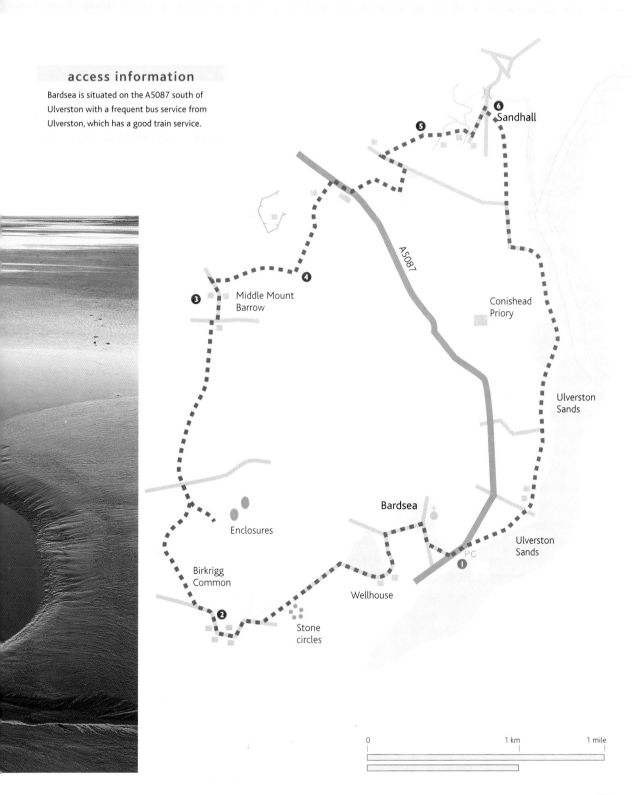

access information

Bardsea is situated on the A5087 south of
Ulverston with a frequent bus service from
Ulverston, which has a good train service.

Sandhall

A5087

Middle Mount
Barrow

Conishead
Priory

Ulverston
Sands

Bardsea

Enclosures

Ulverston
Sands

PC

Birkrigg
Common

Wellhouse

Stone
circles

| 0 | | 1 km | 1 mile |

▲ Map: Explorer OL 7
▲ Distance: 6.44 km/4 miles
▲ Walk ID: 447 William Kembery

Difficulty rating

Time

▲ Hills or Fells, Sea, Pub, Great Views

Arnside from Arnside Knott

From Arnside Knott, the walk passes through some woodland then drops down to the shoreline and along the promenade. After a stroll through the village the walk leads back up to visit the summit of the Knott for glorious views across Morecambe Bay.

1 Go to the kissing gate in the wall of the car park. Head downhill through the trees until a major path crosses and then turn right. Go through the mini-gate and go straight over a crossing path and a ladder stile. Follow the fenced path to the road. Turn left and go down the lane. Just before a life-belt, bear right to join the main path around New Barn's Bay. Continue along the shore to enter the trees beside another life-belt.

2 Follow the footpath to a gate, and climb the stile. Follow the left-hand boundary to reach another stile by the boatyard and cross it to join the shore again. Continue along the path into Arnside. Pass the station and take a track to the right signposted Silverdale Road.

3 Cross Silverdale Road going slightly left to find an opening into a narrow ginnel. Go along this ginnel, then round some garages. Go up a path climbing steeply up to emerge through a gap in a wall onto Higher Knott Road.

4 Cross the road and take a footpath signposted The Knott. Pass through the iron kissing gate and follow the footpath away, to arrive at a gate. Bear left to visit the summit. Walk up the hill keeping the wall on the left, and when a gate is seen in this wall, bear away to the right where the path splits into two. Head for the wicker gate seen in the wall ahead.

5 Go through it and take the right-hand path, climbing uphill. Ignore all paths off until eventually arriving at the stone bench. Head back slightly right on a clear path, uphill to the trig point. Now return to the bench and go forward on a clear path going downhill. Ignore all minor paths off until a fork is reached and the path splits into two good paths. Take the right-hand path and go through a gate in a wall to reach a viewpoint.

6 Turn left and follow the footpath down the hill with a wall over on the left to eventually meet the wall at a gap. Turn right and follow the good path through the trees, keeping right on a good track to arrive at the car park.

further information

Morecambe Bay sands can be extremely treacherous. In the summer you can walk across safely, but only in the company of The Queen's Guide to the Sands, a traditional office held by an experienced local guide. At very high tides the beach section of this walk may not be passable.

There are some wonderful sites to visit around Morecambe Bay. At Heysham, you can see St Patrick's Chapel, where the saint is said to have been shipwrecked on his way to Scotland in the 5th century.

Arnside is on the B5282, off the A6 at
Milnthorpe. It is easily reached from the M6,
junctions 35 or 36. Arnside Knott car park is
well signposted from the town, past the
youth hostel. Trains run from Lancaster and
Barrow-in-Furness. Buses run from Kendal.

▲ Map: Explorer OL 4

▲ Distance: 6 km/3¾ miles

▲ Walk ID: 173 David Stewart

Difficulty rating

Time

▲ Hills or Fells, Lake/Loch, Pub, Toilets, Church, National Trust/NTS, Birds, Great Views

Lake Buttermere

A charming walk that takes you on a circuit of Lake Buttermere, one of the prettiest and most isolated of the Lakes. The lake itself nestles at the end of its valley, with the steep sides of Red Pike, High Stile and High Crag rising up directly from it.

1 Pass down to the left of the Fish Inn and head for the lake. Immediately, you can see the waters of Sour Milk Gill cascading down the hillside. Head towards the waterfall, ignoring the path signed to Scale Force on your right.

2 As you reach the lake edge bear right and make straight for the base of the fall. From here it is a truly impressive sight, especially after a good rainfall. Turn left to follow the lakeside, taking the path which runs right by the water's edge. It is very difficult to go wrong, so all you need do is soak up the glorious scenery.

3 After a kilometre or so, the path runs beyond the end of the lake, and you will see a track to the left passing over Peggy's Bridge in the direction of Gatesgarth Farm. Follow the track, taking time to stop at the bridge, where you can admire the spectacular view along the lake. Continue up to the farm.

4 Turn left onto the road. There is a short stretch on tarmac here, but it is a quiet route. Shortly you come to a small bay and the lakeside path forks away from the road. The path follows closely along the lake edge.

5 Before you reach the village again, pass through a short tunnel hewn into the rock (mind your head as the sign here warns!).

6 Once you get beyond the lake, follow the well-signed paths back to the village.

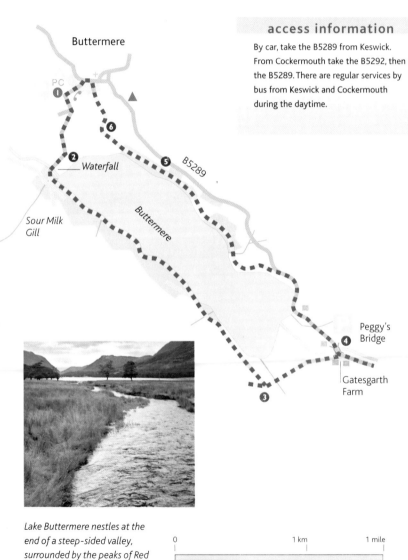

access information

By car, take the B5289 from Keswick. From Cockermouth take the B5292, then the B5289. There are regular services by bus from Keswick and Cockermouth during the daytime.

Lake Buttermere nestles at the end of a steep-sided valley, surrounded by the peaks of Red Pike, High Stile and High Crag.

0   1 km   1 mile

▲ Map: Explorer OL 7
▲ Distance: 6 km/3¾ miles
▲ Walk ID: 1299 Gary Gray

Difficulty rating

Time

▲ Lake/Loch, Pub, National Trust/NTS, Wildlife, Birds, Flowers, Great Views

Black Crag from Tarn Hows

This is a very pleasant, easy-to-follow, linear walk along Tarn Hows and up to Black Crag. The fantastic views include a panorama of nearly all the major fells.

❶ From the car park walk out onto the road. The path down to the tarn is straight ahead. Take the right-hand fork towards the tarn. On reaching the gate, go through and follow the path alongside the tarn.

❷ At the signpost (Arnside and Langdale), turn left. This is part of the Cumbrian way. This track leads you away from the tarn. On reaching a gate and stile, turn right onto a stone track. There are fine views of Tarn Hows to the right about two-thirds of the way up.

❸ When you reach the plantation of Iron Keld on your left, look for a gate and a signpost marked 'Iron Keld'. Turn left through the gate and follow the track through the plantation.

❹ As you emerge from the plantation, you will reach a gate and swing gate. Go through and walk on for a short way through an old set of stone gateposts. A path joins from the right at a sharp angle. Take this path which first doubles back then soon swings up to the left and towards the fell. Follow the grassy track upwards.

❺ On reaching the summit there is a trig point at the top. You can continue over the stile and along the fell. However, there is no way down and you must return to the stile and the track. For your return journey, simply head back the way you came.

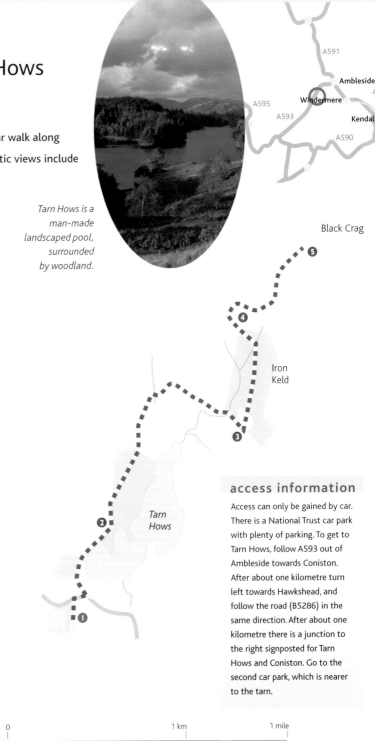

Tarn Hows is a man-made landscaped pool, surrounded by woodland.

Black Crag

Iron Keld

Tarn Hows

access information

Access can only be gained by car. There is a National Trust car park with plenty of parking. To get to Tarn Hows, follow A593 out of Ambleside towards Coniston. After about one kilometre turn left towards Hawkshead, and follow the road (B5286) in the same direction. After about one kilometre there is a junction to the right signposted for Tarn Hows and Coniston. Go to the second car park, which is nearer to the tarn.

0   1 km   1 mile

▲ Map: Explorer OL 7
▲ Distance: 11.27 km/7 miles
▲ Walk ID: 1268 Harold Toze

Difficulty rating

Time

▲ Hills or Fells, River, Lake/Loch, Pub, Toilets, Wildlife, Great Views, Gift Shop, Industrial Archaeology, Tea Shop, Waterfall, Woodland

Skelwith Bridge from Elterwater

This is a low-level walk with many interesting features to look out for along the way, including two waterfalls – Colwith Force and Skelwith Force – and an old clapper bridge at Slater Bridge.

1 From the car park entrance turn left to cross the bridge. Go along the road and take the lane that forks off to the right. Continue on the rough track. Go over the hill and down to the minor road through Little Langdale.

2 At the road junction cross diagonally down a farm track. At the farm buildings follow the footpath alongside the stone wall. Cross Slater Bridge and go up the track on the other side through a stile onto a wider track. Turn left and follow the stream. Go along the track ahead to the next footbridge/ford.

3 Follow the track away from the ford up the slope to the right. Follow the left fork signposted Skelwith and Colwith. Continue uphill to Stang End and along the road to High Park Farm. After the farm take the path leading off to the left. Go across the field and through a gate. Follow a small footpath downhill to arrive at Colwith Force waterfall. Continue alongside the stream to come out on a minor road. Turn right and after about 100 m there is a footpath signposted to Skelwith Bridge.

4 Turn left on to the footpath. At Park Farm take the right-hand path to the bridge. The path continues parallel to the road, eventually joining it. Continue down the main road to Skelwith Bridge. At the bottom of the hill turn left crossing the river by the road bridge.

Skelwith Force is a short distance up the stream. Pass by the Skelwith Bridge Hotel to the junction of the B5343 and the A593. Cross the B5343 coming from the left and go up the minor road. At the top of the hill turn right along the Ambleside Road, then almost immediately left on a minor road. Turn right again at another minor road, which is marked to Loughrigg Tarn only.

5 Pass Dillygarth Cottage and turn left along a rough track. Follow the track around the north side of Loughrigg Tarn. At the Howe turn left through a wooden gate and down the hill to pass near to the end of Loughrigg Tarn. At the minor road turn left. Soon a track leads off to the right, signed back to Skelwith Bridge. Take this track, passing Crag Head Cottage on the left. Just before the dry-stone wall turn right and at the top of the next rise Elterwater should come into view through the trees. Continue downhill and go through a stile in the stone wall into the wood beyond. You will reach Langdale Road.

6 Cross Langdale Road diagonally and hop over the low wall alongside the wooden gate. Follow the track down the slope to join the main track beside Elterwater and continue along this track to return to the car park.

access information

Elterwater is on the B5343 to the west of Ambleside. There are two car parks in Elterwater. This walk starts from the lower car park.

The peaks of the spectacular Langdale Valley, which include Pavey Ark, Pike o'Stickle and Bow Fell, are a popular destination for hill-walkers.

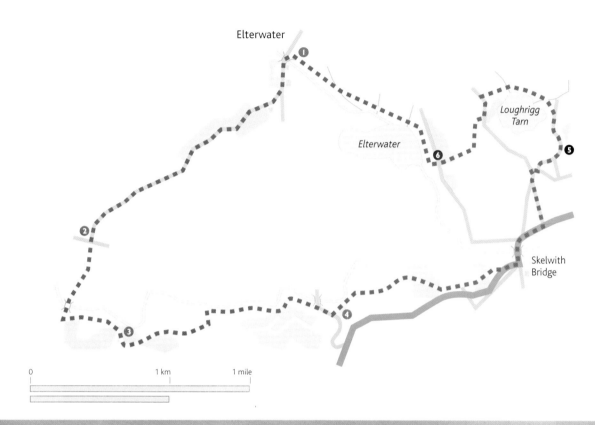

Elterwater

Loughrigg Tarn

Elterwater

Skelwith Bridge

0   1 km   1 mile

▲ Map: Explorer 265
▲ Distance: 9 km/5½ miles
▲ Walk ID: 342 Jim Grindle

Difficulty rating

Time

▲ River, Pub, Toilets, Play Area, Wildlife, Flowers, Great Views, Good for Wheelchairs

Loggerheads and the Leete Path

Liverpool
Birkenhead
M53
Holywell
A55
Chester
Mold
A483
A494
Wrexham

Loggerheads is not far from Mold and is a Country Park. The walk takes you through the park and along a terrace above the River Alyn. Field paths and country lanes bring you back to the Leete Path near the start.

❶ Cross the little bridge at the end of the car park. Pass by some buildings and continue to a stone bridge over the River Alyn. Go over the bridge and turn left towards a gate at the end of the country park signposted Leete Path. The gravelled track becomes muddier and the channel of the Leete is to your right. Pass the boarding kennels and continue on their driveway past a white metal gate to a lane. Cross to another signpost.

❷ You come to a diagonal crossing of tracks. Take the north-west path that keeps you on the same level. You will notice a number of mine shafts on the right and will shortly cross a bridge over the largest shaft. Another diagonal crossroads is reached and then a signposted junction with another right of way.

❸ Following this you come to a lane. Turn left, downhill, and cross the road bridge. On a sharp right bend, follow the footpath sign to Pentre on the left.

❹ Cross six stiles, keeping to the left-hand edge of the fields. The seventh takes you to the other side of the wire and the next down to a junction with a bridleway. Turn right and go up the hill with the cascade from a small lake on your left. You come to a lane where you turn left. Pass Wayside Cottage and turn left at the T-junction.

❺ Walk for about 2 km, then look right to see the Jubilee Tower on Moel Fammau. Continue until a concrete road to the left takes you down to a ford and bridge. Cross the river and climb towards a signpost 'Leete Path, Loggerheads' on the right, just where the lane bends left.

❻ Take the right turn, and retrace your steps to the car park, 1.5 km away.

This footpath leads you through such tranquil countryside that it is difficult to believe that the area was once an industrial landscape of mine-shafts, waterwheels and the water channel called the Leete.

access information

Loggerheads Country Park lies 5 km to the west of Mold on the A494. Parking is by the Information Centre. The Ruthin/Mold bus service calls in at the car park.

further information

The Leete was a clay-lined channel, designed to carry water that had been pumped from the lead mines in the adjacent valley to prevent flooding. It runs alongside the River Alyn for a distance of about 5 kilometres.

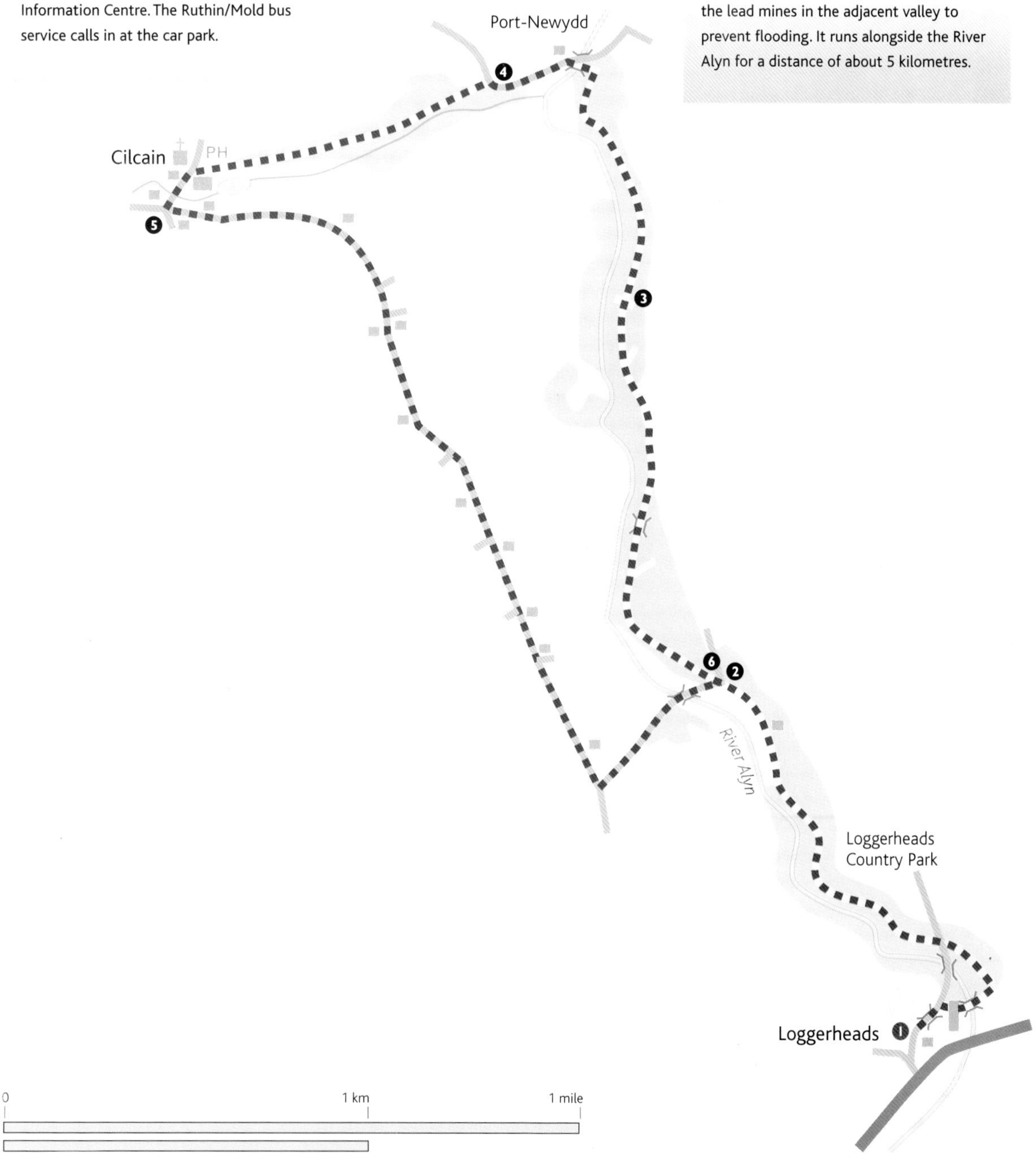

Port-Newydd

4

Cilcain

PH

5

3

6 **2**

River Alyn

Loggerheads
Country Park

Loggerheads **1**

0   1 km   1 mile

▲ Map: Explorer 256

▲ Distance: 9 km/5½ miles

▲ Walk ID: 230 Jim Grindle

Difficulty rating

Time

▲ River, Toilets, National Trust/NTS, Good for Wheelchairs (accessible for part of the way)

Erddig Hall at Wrexham Steeple

This is a short, pleasant walk through the grounds surrounding Erddig Hall, a National Trust property. It includes riverside, parkland and woodland sections and is mostly easy underfoot.

1 Come out of the car park and turn right. Walk towards the crossroads. Go straight across, as far as a signpost by the railings on the left. Join a newly tarred track downhill. After passing a cattle grid you will see the Cup and Saucer Waterfall to your left. Continue on the track, crossing over a bridge. The path will then lead you on to a second, larger bridge.

Erddig Hall provides a majestic backdrop to this footpath, which runs through the grounds that surround the house.

access information

Erddig Hall is 3 km south of
Wrexham and is well signposted
from the A483 and the A525.

further information

The tower of the Parish Church
of St Giles in Wrexham is among
the Seven Wonders of Wales. It is
a short drive from Erddig Hall.

❷ Cross the bridge and go through the
kissing gate on the right. Follow the track
by the river to reach a car park on a lane.
Turn right on to the lane, and just before
the road signs, turn left through a gate.
❸ Follow the river bank or the hedge
on the left of the fields. Watch out for
a footbridge to cross. Follow the white
arrows on the signposts, which lead you
gradually above the river, but stay in the
wood with the river below you on the
right. Cross a bridge and stile near the
edge of the wood and follow the track
to the edge of a meadow.
❹ Make for the large tree. If you look
upwards you will see another signpost
just past a second tree, a large oak. At

the top of the slope keep to the right
edge of the field – the exit is through a
stile to the right.
❺ Cross the stile to the lane, turn left
and cross to a kissing gate. Continue on
the narrow path ahead with fields on
your left. You will reach a signpost. Keep
straight ahead until you come to the end
of the fields on the left. Turn left where
the paths meet. Go left again, still with
the fields on your left and the grounds
of Erddig on your right.
❻ Keep on the path until you come to a
gate. Turn right and go through another
gate. You will see ahead of you the
dovecote by the car park as you return
to the start of the walk.

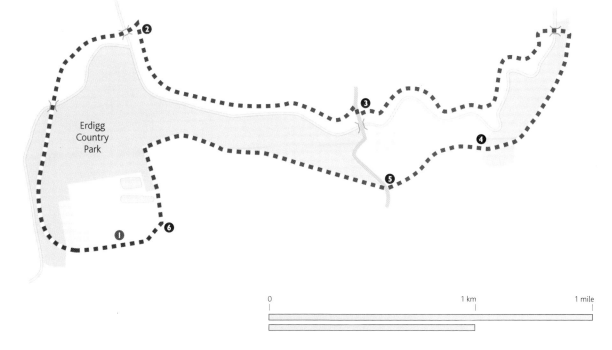

0   1 km   1 mile

▲ Map: Explorer OL 17
▲ Distance: 14 km/8¾ miles
▲ Walk ID: 338 Haydn Williams

Difficulty rating

Time

▲ Pub, Castle, Great Views

Tal-y-Fan

This walk takes you over the northern part of the Carneddau range. Allow yourself time at the summit to enjoy this glorious landscape and also views of Anglesey, Liverpool and the Conwy Valley.

❶ From the car park follow the black track for half a kilometre. The way the tracks diverge is slightly confusing, but you should turn sharp right and follow the obvious track uphill. Keep the lake to your right and continue for half a kilometre, to meet a farmer's track.

❷ Turn right on to this track and stay on it until you reach a wall on the left, following it for about 2.5 km. Cross the ford, then continue uphill, keeping the wall on the right for 200 m. Pick up the track immediately ahead. Continue for about one kilometre, from where you will see a wall 90 degrees to your right.

❸ Turning right at this wall, and by keeping it on your left, you will start a steep climb for 200 m. On reaching the summit cross the ladder stile to the trig point.

❹ At the summit enjoy the extensive views of the Menai Straits, Anglesey, Puffin Island, Conwy Bay, Great Orme, Llandudno Bay, Conwy Castle and Conwy Valley. Recross the ladder stile and go directly downhill with the wall at your back. When you reach a small cairn, turn right on to a footpath that takes you back to the wall. Follow this until you reach a distinct corner of the wall.

❺ From this point pick your own path down to the quarry heading diagonally right for half a kilometre. At the quarry take the left-hand route down. After approximately 200 m a stream drops off to the right. Continue straight on and turn right at the next obvious path.

❻ Walk past the standing stone and this path will bring you back to your original track. Turn left and follow the track back to the car park.

The windswept ridges of the Welsh mountains offer panoramic views to take the breath away.

access information

Conwy is on the A55 near Llandudno. By car from Conwy town square, turn left before the arch, proceed uphill to another arch and follow the road to the right, going uphill for 2 km. Go over the cattle grid and, ignoring the small car park by the road junction, carry on uphill. After a bend on the road you will see a well-built wall with a parking sign. Turn left here into the car park. To come by public transport use the Sherpa Park & Ride.

Pengychnant

1

Craigytedwen

2

From the highest point of this walk you will have excellent views of Conwy, with its magnificent castle and a bridge (below) built to complement the style of the fortress.

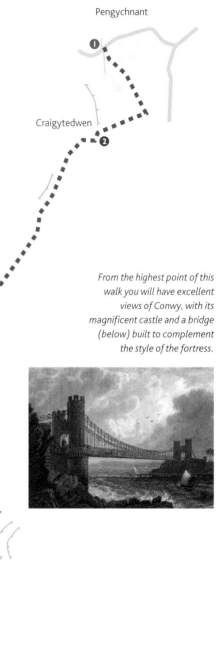

6

Standing Stone

5

Tal-y-Fan

4

3

```
0                    1 km           1 mile
```

▲ Map: Explorer OL 23
▲ Distance: 6 km/3¾ miles
▲ Walk ID: 225 Ian Morison

Difficulty rating

Time

▲ Hills or Fells, Lake/Loch, Toilets, Wildlife, Birds, Great Views

The Precipice Walk, north of Dolgellau

A classic Snowdonia walk with wonderful vistas over the Arans, Coed y Brenin Forest, the Mawddach estuary and Cader Idris. The view is one of the most beautiful panoramas in Wales, and there are perfect spots for picnics.

❶ Turn left out of the car park and follow the minor road for a short way. Turn left along the signposted track. Follow it round to the right where the track splits into two, keeping the open field to your left. Bear left as you pass the stone cottage.

❷ Cross a low ladder stile into woodland and turn right along the path. Cross the stile at the end of the wood into the open country. Follow the path round to the right. Llyn Cynwch is seen down the valley on the left.

❸ Turn right at the corner of the field following the signpost direction. Cross the ladder stile. The village of Llanfachreth is seen in the valley to your right. As you follow the stony path round to the left, Coed y Brenin Forest stretches out in front of you.

❹ The narrow path takes you along the flanks of Foel Cynwch. To the right lies the River Mawddach. The view opens out with the Mawddach estuary becoming visible to the right with distant views of Cader Idris.

❺ Climb over a ladder stile and follow the path round the hillside to the left. Cross a further ladder stile. Follow the path down towards Llyn Cynwch.

❻ Bear left, and drop on to the path by the lake. Follow the path beside the lake. Rejoin the outward route and retrace your steps to the car park.

access information

By car only. A National Park car park is on the left-hand side of the minor road between Dolgellau, on the A470, and the village of Llanfachreth – from Dolgellau, follow signs to the Precipice Walk.

further information

The route runs high above the River Mawddach. The ground drops steeply into the valley so young children will need to be well supervised, but there are no sheer drops. The path is good, but occasionally rocky.

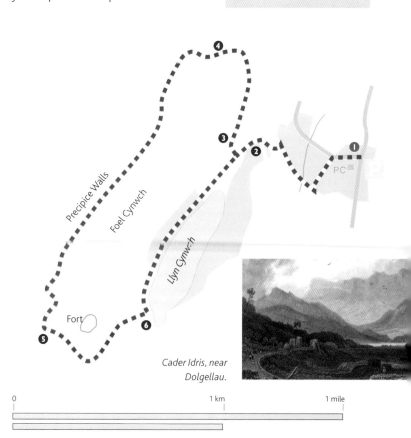

Cader Idris, near Dolgellau.

▲ Map: Explorer OL 17
▲ Distance: 8 km/5 miles
▲ Walk ID: 738 Jim Grindle

Difficulty rating

Time

▲ National Trust/NTS, Great Views, Toilets

Bodnant Gardens & Moel Gyffylog

This walk begins at the attractive National Trust gardens at Bodnant. It covers the unclassified lanes to the east, rising to 250 m and offering outstanding views over the Conwy valley to the Carneddau range.

❶ Turn left out of the car park at Bodnant. In 300 m you will come to a lane, Ffordd Bodnant. Turn left here and left again at the T-junction just ahead. The lane goes uphill for 1.4 km to a junction just past Bodnant Ucha farm.

❷ Turn right. In 350 m you reach a junction with another lane. Turn left here. Pass a junction with a lane from the left and continue to a small farm, Erw Goch. Barely 100 m further on there is another T-junction.

❸ Turn right with the telephone lines on your right. At the top of the rise is another farm and 100 m beyond it you reach another T-junction. Turn left and go only 50 m, to a lane coming in from the right.

❹ Turn right here for the next junction, 800 m away. Turn right at the signpost in the direction of Eglwysbach. It is 2.5 km downhill to the village, and you cross the stream by the entrance to Gyffylog farm on the way.

❺ Turn right in Eglwysbach, to pass a bus stop on the left and a chapel on the right. Eight hundred metres from the junction you reach a red telephone box and a bus shelter by a crossroads in the hamlet of Graig. Bodnant is signposted on the right. Keep straight on, passing the bus shelter on your left.

❻ Follow the road to Bodnant, to visit the gardens or return to the car park.

further information

The café, car park and the garden centre are free to enter but there is an entrance fee to the gardens themselves (NT members go in free). In addition to the beautiful gardens, there are many semi-wild areas and ponds. The grounds are open every day from mid-March to early November.

access information

Bodnant is on the A470 south of Llandudno and is well signposted from the A55. A bus from Conwy stops outside the gardens.

This walk starts at the lovely gardens at Bodnant.

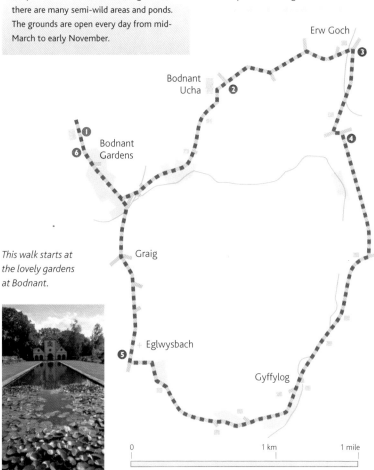

▲ Map: Explorer OL 17
▲ Distance: 6 km/3¾ miles
▲ Walk ID: 772 Hadyn Williams

Difficulty rating

Time

▲ Mountains, Lake/Loch, Great Views

Beddgelert Forest

This walk through Beddgelert Forest gives great views of the surrounding mountains. It is easy to follow the route with the aid of the numbered marker poles set at regular intervals through the forest.

1 At the top of the car park, take a shortcut to the track, through the bushes. Turn left on to the track. Turn right at the first junction, at marker pole 80. Follow the delightful little stream on your right. On your right you have views of Moel Hebog. Turn right on to the concrete bridge. Straight ahead are views of Y Garn.

2 Look for marker pole 64 and turn left. There is a view of Yr Aran. Carry on uphill keeping the stream on your right. Ahead is the Nantlle Ridge, on the left is Moel Hebog and Moel Ogof.

3 Turn left at the T-junction and cross a concrete bridge. Turn sharp right on to a footpath, ignoring the junction ahead. Look for a marker pole 66. Bear left on to the track at marker pole 34. Take the path to the right. Bear left at the junction, cross over a concrete bridge at marker pole 42, and carry straight on, ignoring the turning to the right.

4 Keep bearing left, ignoring the track on your right and the grassy path ahead. Turn left and go downhill at the junction at marker pole 36.

5 Carry on downhill. Turn right on to the main track, passing marker pole 35. Pass marker pole 34 on your left.

6 Turn left at the junction, heading downhill. Directly ahead is Moel Hebog, marked by marker pole 33. Turn right at the junction marked by marker pole 70.

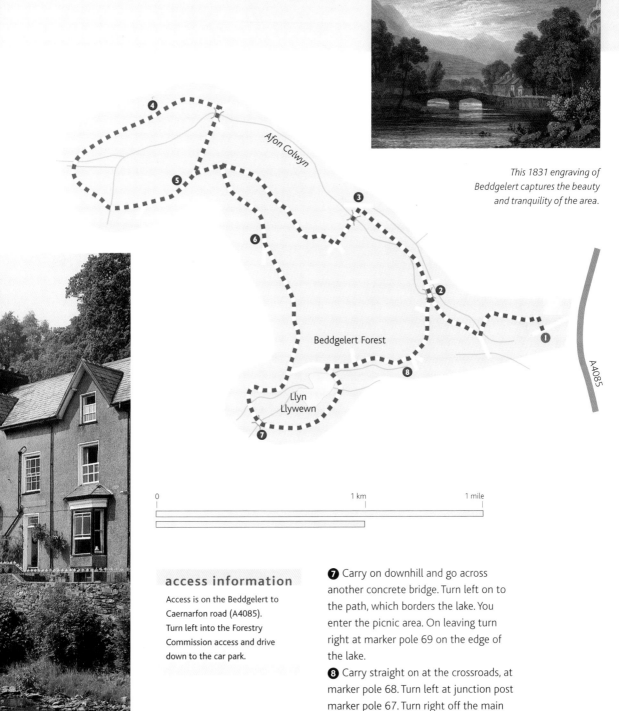

This 1831 engraving of Beddgelert captures the beauty and tranquility of the area.

Afon Colwyn

A4085

Beddgelert Forest

Llyn Llywewn

0		1 km	1 mile

access information

Access is on the Beddgelert to Caernarfon road (A4085). Turn left into the Forestry Commission access and drive down to the car park.

The village of Beddgelert, at the confluence of the Glaslyn and Colwyn rivers, is also situated at the approaches to two mountain passes, offering access to some of the most spectacular scenery in Snowdonia.

7 Carry on downhill and go across another concrete bridge. Turn left on to the path, which borders the lake. You enter the picnic area. On leaving turn right at marker pole 69 on the edge of the lake.

8 Carry straight on at the crossroads, at marker pole 68. Turn left at junction post marker pole 67. Turn right off the main track by the trees, marker pole 65, and down the cinder path. Turn right just before the concrete bridge sending you down on the path you came up on. Turn left at marker pole 80 and proceed back to the car park.

▲ Map: Explorer 255
▲ Distance: 6 km/3¾ miles
▲ Walk ID: 1015 Jim Grindle

Difficulty rating

Time

▲ Hills or Fells, Mountains, River,
Toilets, Great Views, Food Shop, Moor,
Tea Shop, Waterfall

Pistyll Llanrhaeadr and the Berwyns

Starting at a waterfall, this short, circular walk takes you into the fringes of
the Berwyn Mountains, where there are clear views of the craggy eastern faces
of the highest peaks.

❶ Go through the small wooden gate
by the café and turn right towards the
falls. Turn right into the woods. Pass
through a gate and follow the path
slightly left to a stile and gate at the
edge of the wood.

❷ Follow the stony track to the steps.
At the top, turn left. Look for a signpost
on the left of the track. It points towards
a ladder stile. To go to the falls turn left
and return to continue the walk. Further
up the valley the path divides.

❸ Take the lower path, on the left. The
path ends but carry on to a very straight
and deep stream bed. On the far side is a
wire fence. Turn left, downhill to where
the stream joins the main stream. Go
downstream to where the water is
shallower. Cross, turn right and make for
the corner where the two fences meet.

❹ Cross the gate and turn left. Go to
the left of the sheep pens and then turn
right, following a little stream uphill until
you can cross it. At the conifer trees,
cross the gate and follow the fence on
your left. At the top of this first rise
there are good views of the Berwyns.

❺ Keep going with the fence on your
left. The track eventually rises to the
highest point of the walk. It then drops
again and takes a sharp turn left in the
first of a series of bends into the valley
on your left. At the bend leave the track,
using sheep tracks to reach a path

alongside a fence below you. Aim for the
rowan tree. Now turn left and follow the
path along the fence. Pass a stile on your
right and you will come to another one
leading into a wood.

❻ Follow the path through woodland
and some small clearings until you see
some fencing on the right below you.
You will soon come back to the iron
bridge. Cross it to get back to the gate.

*The remote peaks of the
Berwyns are wild and deserted,
populated only by grazing
mountain sheep.*

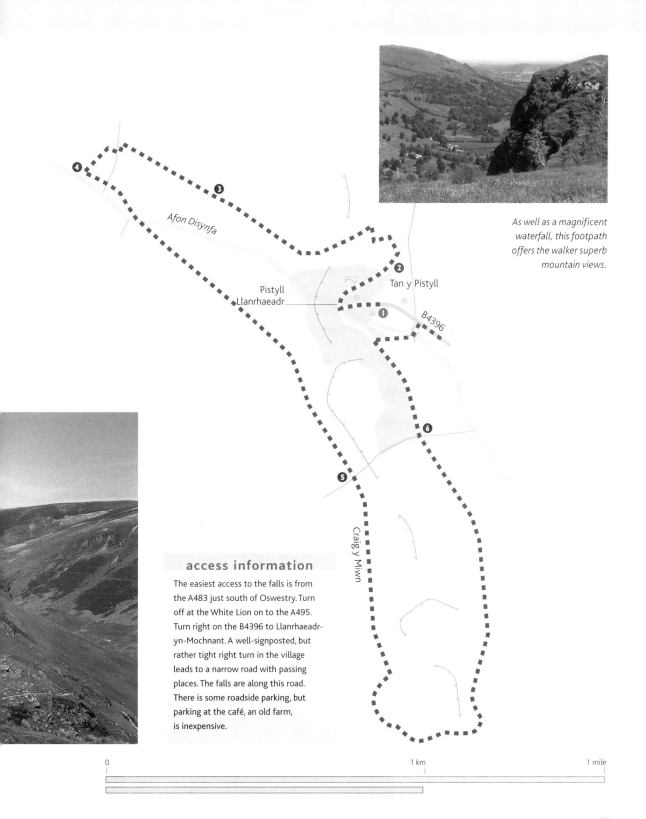

As well as a magnificent
waterfall, this footpath
offers the walker superb
mountain views.

4

3

Afon Disynfa

2

PC

Tan y Pistyll

Pistyll
Llanrhaeadr

1

B4396

6

5

Craig y Mwn

access information

The easiest access to the falls is from
the A483 just south of Oswestry. Turn
off at the White Lion on to the A495.
Turn right on the B4396 to Llanrhaeadr-
yn-Mochnant. A well-signposted, but
rather tight right turn in the village
leads to a narrow road with passing
places. The falls are along this road.
There is some roadside parking, but
parking at the café, an old farm,
is inexpensive.

0   1 km   1 mile

▲ Map: Explorer 265
▲ Distance: 4 km/2½ miles
▲ Walk ID: 1567 Jim Grindle

Difficulty rating

Time

▲ Lake/Loch, Toilets, Museum, Church, Good for Wheelchairs, Café, Food Shop, Good for Kids, Nature Trail, Restaurant, Woodland, Ancient Monument.

St Winetride's Well from Holywell

This walk in Greenfield Heritage Park includes St Winefride's Well, one of the Seven Wonders of Wales. There is one main track running through the park. Smaller paths lead to the old railway and industrial sites.

1 From the car park take the signposted path towards the Visitor Centre. Just before you reach the centre there is a path going off to the right. Follow this path. On the right there is a garden on the site of the Abbey Wire Mill. Continue on the path to the left until you reach a reservoir.

2 Take the fork to the right so that you keep by the edge of the water. A little further on the path divides. Take the right fork and stay on the path until you have to go up left to the railway track. The railway track is the level path on the right. Stay on this until you see some gravelled steps going down to the right.

3 Take the little path down the steps and stay on it until you have to go up left to the railway. Take the right branch, which is the old railway track. Look for a flight of steps going up to the left, but ignore them to stay on the track. Watch now for a split in this track.

4 Take the right fork at a red and white marker post 8JF. Just out of sight is a small gate by a larger one. Go through the small gate and drop down through an industrial area to the B5121. You will see a footpath sign on the left of the opening on to the road. Turn left.

5 About 100 m up the road is the entrance to St Winefride's Well. After visiting the famous well, go back the

way you came and stay on the old railway track. This will bring you right back to Basingwerk Abbey, passing by features you have passed earlier. The track takes you over a little bridge and then it curves down to the left to the ruins of the abbey.

6 Go through the little gate to the abbey. At the far end is a similar gate. The car park is also signposted.

further information

Wheelchairs can be used for this walk by omitting the sections with steps – all the paths join up again on the old railway.

The estuaries of North Wales can provide some of the most spectacular views in Britain.

access information

Holywell lies between the A55 Expressway
and the A548; both Basingwerk Abbey and
St Winefride's Well are signposted. Buses
from Chester to Rhyl call at Holywell.
The car park on the B5121 is closest to the
Visitor Centre, but the car park on the A548
for the abbey can also be used.

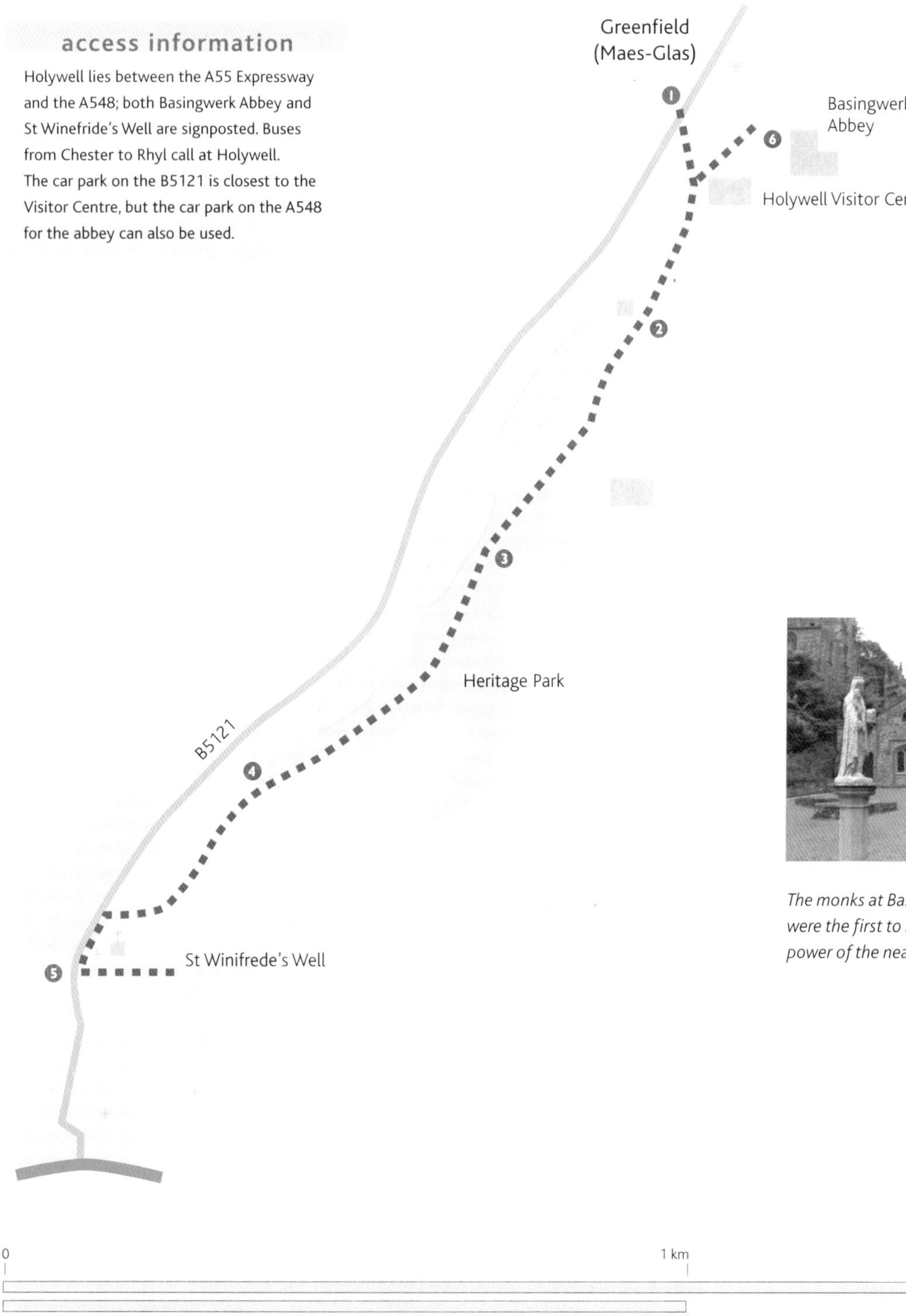

Basingwerk
Abbey

Holywell Visitor Centre

Heritage Park

B5121

St Winifrede's Well

The monks at Basingwerk Abbey
were the first to harness the
power of the nearby stream.

0   1 km   1 mile

▲ Map: Explorer 287
▲ Distance: 10 km/6¼ miles
▲ Walk ID: 1123 William Kembery

Difficulty rating

Time

▲ Pub, Toilets, Castle, National Trust/
NTS, Flowers, Great Views, Food Shop,
Good for Kids, Moor, Nature Trail, Tea
Shop, Woodland, Ancient Monument

Rivington Pike and Lever Park

Explore the many facets of Lever Park and seek out the half-hidden formal garden, the towers, the barns and a splendid folly of a castle.

❶ From Lowehouse car park, go over the stile. Follow the path to the bridge. Cross and turn right to another stile. Cross and follow the path. Go over the next stile, turning sharp left to join a path and walking downhill to continue straight on down a track. Follow this track. When a junction of tracks is reached a kissing gate can be seen on the left.

❷ Go through the gate and either follow the 'garden trail' up the hill or go directly up to Pigeon Tower via the flight of steps. Behind the tower go through the bridlegate and on to the wide track. Go through the kissing gate on the left and ascend Rivington Pike by any path.

❸ Turn right (across the front of the tower) and take the footpath that leads downhill. The track broadens out. At the next junction go straight across through the little gate and follow the grassy bridleway downhill. Go past the farm track. At the next junction, turn right (not sharp right). Follow this to a junction, before a gate ahead. Turn left downhill. At the main road, cross and head for Bridleway Castle. As the track swings right, carry straight on up.

❹ At the T-junction turn left. With the castle in view, follow the track round, turning right all the time. Beyond the castle, turn left away through the trees. At a junction of paths take the left fork and follow it parallel to the reservoir.

❺ At the fork take the left-hand path and follow along the banks of the reservoir, across the bridge to the small school car park. Turn left and at the main road turn right along it. Follow the road round to the right until you reach a footpath on the right signposted to the Great House Information Centre. Take this path through the woods, parallel to the road. Pass the arboretum and go towards the centre.

❻ Cross the main road and follow the path signed 'Rivington Hall Barn' alongside a wide road. Just before the hall gates, turn right on to a good track and follow it round to the back of the hall. Turn left, retracing the way out to arrive at the car park.

access information

Lowehouse car park is reached by taking the A675 north from Bolton, turning left in Belmont village, and turning first left after 4.8 km.

The views from Rivington Pike across to the Fylde coast are awe-inspiring. This was one of the heights on which beacons were lit to warn of the approach of the Spanish Armada.

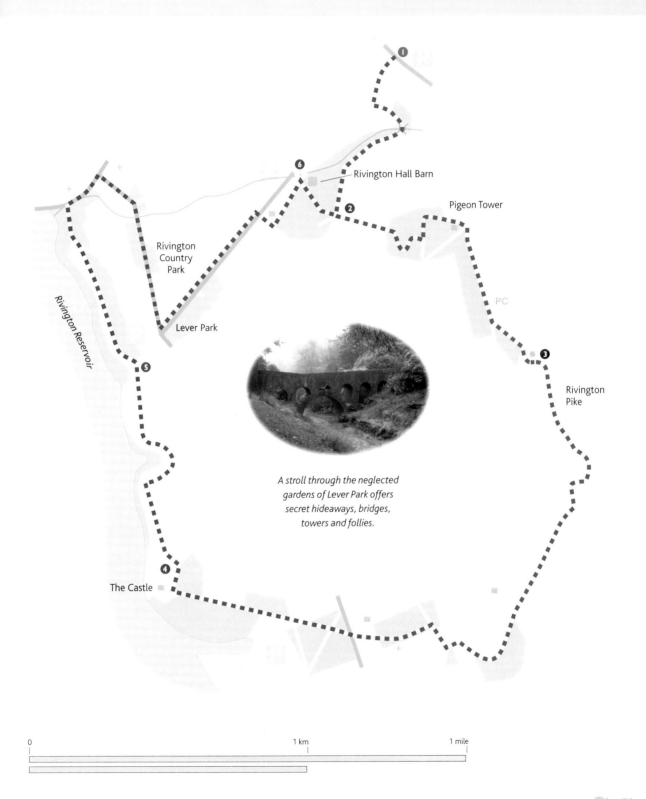

Rivington Hall Barn

Pigeon Tower

Rivington
Country
Park

Lever Park

Rivington Reservoir

PC

Rivington
Pike

The Castle

*A stroll through the neglected
gardens of Lever Park offers
secret hideaways, bridges,
towers and follies.*

| 0 | 1 km | 1 mile |

▲ Map: Explorer 19
▲ Distance: 10 km/6¼ miles
▲ Walk ID: 786 Barry Smith

Difficulty rating

Time
●●●●●

▲ River, Pub, Toilets, Wildlife,
Woodland, Flowers, Good for
Wheelchairs

Tockholes Plantations from Abbey Village

A delightful walk that includes a lovely valley, with some breathtaking views at the start, then enters steep woodland, which includes the Tockholes Plantations. There are bluebells in the spring and early summer, wild garlic, fungi and native trees.

❶ From the corner of the car park, go through the gateposts towards the reservoir. Ignore the stile to the farm on the left. Turn left at the footpath sign next to a house. Follow the track and cross the water run-off, using the bridge if the water is running. Follow the track to the embankment of Roddlesworth Reservoir. Go left at the concrete 'seats'.

❷ At the other end of the embankment, bear right to enter the woodland.
At the next signpost, bear slightly right to go downhill with the path to a gate/stile at the next embankment. Go left with the smaller path.

❸ Keeping to the path by the wall/reservoir, rejoin the main path and turn right. At the next sign/junction for the Visitor Centre, keep straight on and the same at the next, to go slightly downhill once again and come out at a gate/bridge and the River Roddlesworth.

❹ Turn right. Cross the bridge and go through the kissing gate in the wall. Follow the track by the river, in the most delightful part of the walk, over a footbridge and up and down steps, until you come to a fence/bridge where you bear left on a wider track through woods.

❺ Go over a stile and continue straight on to the junction and bear right with the smaller footpath sign, to continue through woodland. When you reach a wall and gap, cross the footbridge and bear left again with the smaller footpath sign, on the path next to the reservoir.

❻ Turn right at the footbridge/sign to come to the concrete seats once again. Turn left and follow the footpath back to the car park at the start.

further information

If you wish to include a visit to Hollinshead Hall it will extend this walk by 2.5 km, but it is well worth the effort. Make the hall your first port of call if you start at Slipper Lowe car park, or the Visitor Centre at Tockholes.

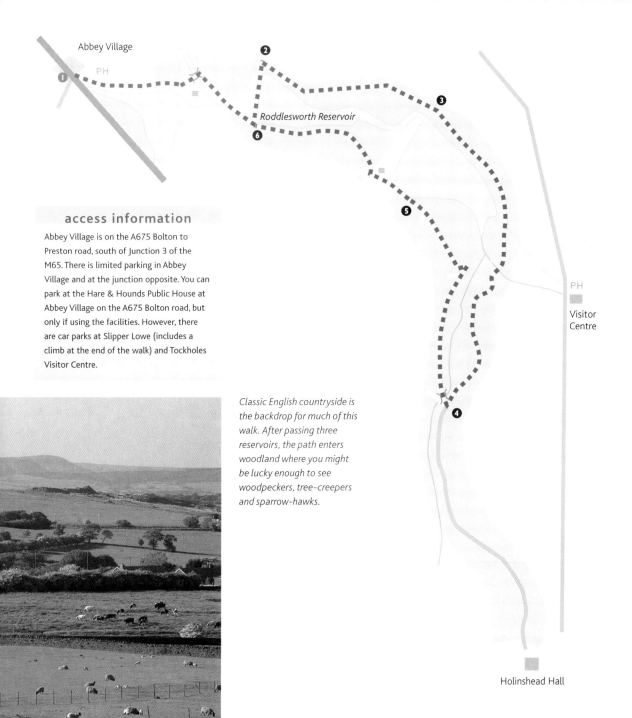

Abbey Village

❶ PH

❷

❸

Roddlesworth Reservoir

❻

❺

❹

PH

Visitor Centre

Holinshead Hall

access information

Abbey Village is on the A675 Bolton to Preston road, south of Junction 3 of the M65. There is limited parking in Abbey Village and at the junction opposite. You can park at the Hare & Hounds Public House at Abbey Village on the A675 Bolton road, but only if using the facilities. However, there are car parks at Slipper Lowe (includes a climb at the end of the walk) and Tockholes Visitor Centre.

Classic English countryside is the backdrop for much of this walk. After passing three reservoirs, the path enters woodland where you might be lucky enough to see woodpeckers, tree-creepers and sparrow-hawks.

0   1 km   1 mile

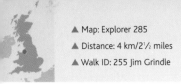

▲ Map: Explorer 285
▲ Distance: 4 km/2½ miles
▲ Walk ID: 255 Jim Grindle

Difficulty rating

Time

▲ Pub, National Trust/NTS, Wildlife

Freshfield and Dobson's Ride

Although this footpath is on the coast, we have classified it as a woodland walk because it is a very quick and easy stroll through tranquil Corsican pine woods. You may be lucky enough to see some of the area's red squirrels.

1 On leaving Freshfield Station turn left, and left again at the telephone box. Walk past the row of shops and then the station car park. At the end of the car park you can continue on the road or branch left on to the bridleway – they join up again further on. The tarmac ends at the last house and becomes a gravelled track.

2 Take the fork left on the wider track following the railway line as far as a level crossing. Go over the railway line and follow the track through a golf course until you reach a metal gate at the entrance to the National Nature Reserve.

3 Take the right fork, passing round the end of the golf course on a winding track until you reach a junction.

4 Go left at this junction, following the signpost for the Sefton Coastal Footpath. In 100 m the sandy path turns right by a white-topped post and in another 50 m it enters the wood. Do not go through the gate on the left – it is 'No Entry'. The track winds through the wood for one

kilometre with white-topped posts to keep you on the right route. At the end of the wood you come to a broad, stony track – Dobson's Ride.

5 Turn right and follow the track for a further kilometre, crossing an open area and then entering the woods again. The path drops a little and you come to a fork with a white post.

6 Stay on the main track by turning left at the white post. In 50 m you will come back to the path to retrace your steps on the outward route.

This is one of the few areas of Britain where you may be able to see the native red squirrel, now an endangered species.

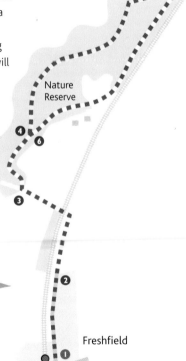

access information

The walk starts at Freshfield Station on the Southport/Liverpool line. Access by road is from the A565. Follow the tourist signs to Formby Point (National Trust). The route crosses the railway line at Freshfield Station where there is parking.

0   1 km   1 mile

▲ Map: Explorer 267

▲ Distance: 6 km/3¾ miles

▲ Walk ID: 234 R. & C. Jones

Difficulty rating

Time

▲ Toilets, Wildlife, Birds, Flowers, Great Views

The Sandstone Trail from Delamere

This walk starts from Delamere Station and follows country roads and the Sandstone Trail within the Delamere Forest. The Sandstone Trail runs from Frodsham in the north to Grindley Brook on the Shropshire border.

❶ Leave the car park and walk towards the railway station entrance. In front of the station turn right and head for the main road. On reaching the main road turn right and walk along the footpath on the other side of the road for about a kilometre. There are good views to the left on a clear day. To the right is a hill on which was once a Saxon hill fort.

❷ On reaching the road junction with Eddisbury Hill turn right, and climb the hill. Continue along this road until you reach the junction with Stoney Lane.

❸ Cross over on to a sandy track and follow the path. You are now on the course of an old Roman road. On reaching the gate cross the stile and enter a large field, keep straight ahead keeping the field boundary on your right, and head for the far right-hand corner of the field. Cross the stile and continue along a path bounded by trees. Cross this stile and enter Nettleford Wood.

❹ On reaching the crossing path turn right on the Sandstone Trail. When you get to the footpath sign keep straight ahead, and cross the stile next to the five-barred gate. Follow the grassy track, which eventually starts to descend.

❺ On reaching the junction with Eddisbury Lodge in front of you, turn right along the road. This will lead you past the Delamere Visitor Centre.

❻ Just past the Visitor Centre is a bridge over the railway. At the side of the bridge is an alleyway, which leads back down to the car park.

access information

This walk starts at Delamere Railway Station. Access by car is via the A556 and then the B5152, which leads to the Lindmere Picnic site adjacent to the station.

A stirring view of Shropshire's beautiful pine forests.

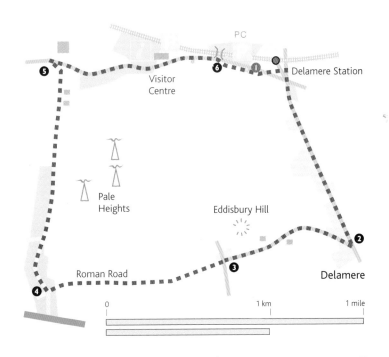

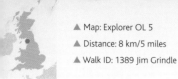

▲ Map: Explorer OL 5
▲ Distance: 8 km/5 miles
▲ Walk ID: 1389 Jim Grindle

Difficulty rating

Time

● ● ● ●

▲ Hills or Fells, Mountains, River,
Toilets, Church, Wildlife, Birds, Flowers,
Great Views, Food Shop, Good for Kids,
Tea Shop

High Rigg in St John's in the Vale

This walk ascends a low ridge among pine trees, first heading north to moorland, followed by a riverside return going south along St John's Beck. The outward route is a little rocky in parts.

1 Leave the car park by the gate at the north end. Turn left on a section of disused road to reach the A591. Turn right, then right again over a ladder stile. Where the path forks go left and in a few moments, at another fork, turn left again. This route goes uphill in a series of short steps among pine trees, taking you through a gap in a stone wall and eventually to a fence with a stile.

2 Take the broad path that curves away from the fence. The path now passes below the highest point of the ridge and goes through a shallow valley before reaching a substantial stone wall. At the junction of two walls is a ladder stile. Cross this and follow the wall up to the col. The land soon becomes marshy and the path swings to the left to avoid it. Once over some stepping stones you will see that the main path goes back again to the right to rejoin the wall.

3 Keeping by the wall brings you to another high point. When the wall drops, it turns sharply to the right. Here you leave it, following the path straight on to the highest point of High Rigg, with its double cairn. It is easier to leave by the way you came up and go around the summit cone. The path directly in front is a shallow dip. Take either path at the fork. Cross a stile, go around to the left and turn to the right on the lane to reach St John's Church.

4 Go past the church, until the lane bends to the left. Drop to a gate and follow a path down to the beck and turn right. Pass one wall where there is a gap by the edge of the beck and you will come to the first of a number of stiles and gates.

5 Go between the fence and the trees. At the end there is a stile just to the right of some sheep pens. Cross the stile and you will soon be following a fence on your left. Keep on by the fence to Sosgill Bridge. You will come to Low Bridge End Farm and have to walk round the back of it.

6 To finish the walk follow the beck again. It enters woodland, which brings you back to the ladder stile. Turn left and left again for the car park.

access information

The Water Board pay-and-display car park at Legburthwaite is on the east side of the A591 Ambleside/Keswick road. A bus service between the two towns calls at the village.

Blencathra, which rises to the east of Keswick, is also known as 'Saddleback' because of its twin peaks, which soar to a height of 868 m.

A double cairn marks the highest point of High Rigg.

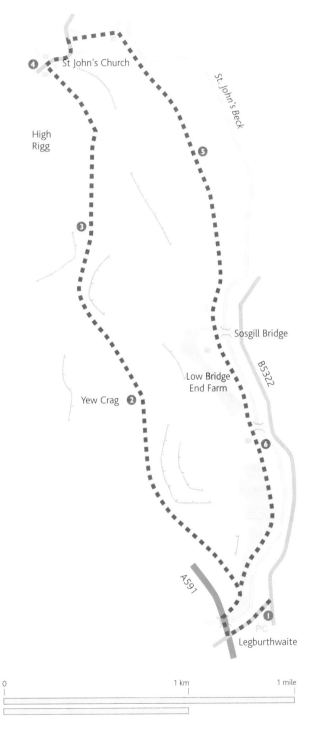

St John's Church

④

High Rigg

St. John's Beck

⑤

③

Sosgill Bridge

Low Bridge End Farm

B5322

Yew Crag ②

⑥

A591

PC

Legburthwaite

0   1 km   1 mile

▲ Map: Explorer OL 4

▲ Distance: 4 km/2½ miles

▲ Walk ID: 933 Craig Lannigan

Difficulty rating

Time

▲ Hills or Fells, Mountains, Lake/Loch, Toilets, Great Views, Food Shop, Moor, Nature Trail, Woodland

Dodd Wood under Ullock Pike

The walk takes you through eerie conifer corridors, which climb gently through Dodd Wood and on to the foothills of Ullock Pike. This allows perfect views of Bassenthwaite Lake and the fells beyond.

❶ From the car park at Mirehouse cross the wooden bridge and follow the footpath that gently rises ahead until you come to a junction with a forest track.

❷ Turn left and begin walking downhill. The path splits into a lower and higher path. Take the right-hand side path, which rises uphill. Follow this path through some lovely isolated pine-canopied aisles.

❸ Turn right at the junction and follow the path that gently rises ahead. Continue along the path, again through tree-lined aisles which are blanketed with pine needles. You will have spectacular views of Bassenthwaite Lake and the fells beyond. To your right is the summit of Skiddaw beyond Ullock Pike. This path comes to an end after a small descent and the path doubles back on itself to the left.

❹ Continue along the gravel track as it gently descends. The path ends once again in a double-back to the left. Follow this path until you reach the main A591. Turn right along the road and walk past the hotel.

❺ Cross over the road to a bus stop next to a series of stone steps descending along a dry-stone wall. Follow the path that bears to the right and cross the stile in front of you to an open field. From the field go over the other stile and follow the path towards a copse of trees. The path then bears to the left and takes you over another three stiles until you reach the road at Green Hill. Turn left and head towards a junction with the A591.

❻ When the Keswick sign appears, turn right and cross over the road. The entrance to a path, which runs alongside the main road, will soon appear. The path ends at a small lay-by and a path ascends ahead towards a gate. Follow it until you come to a junction that takes you down to the bridge you first walked over and back to the car park.

further information

Exploring additional routes around Dodd Wood is well worth the effort, particularly as this route will take under two hours to complete. The nature trails are well marked out and they are very enjoyable.

Bassenthwaite Lake is an expansion of the River Derwent. Surrounded by wooded slopes and fells, it is an ideal centre for rambling and watersports.

Mirehouse is on the A591 north of Keswick. There is a regular bus service from Keswick, stopping at Mirehouse. Parking is limited.

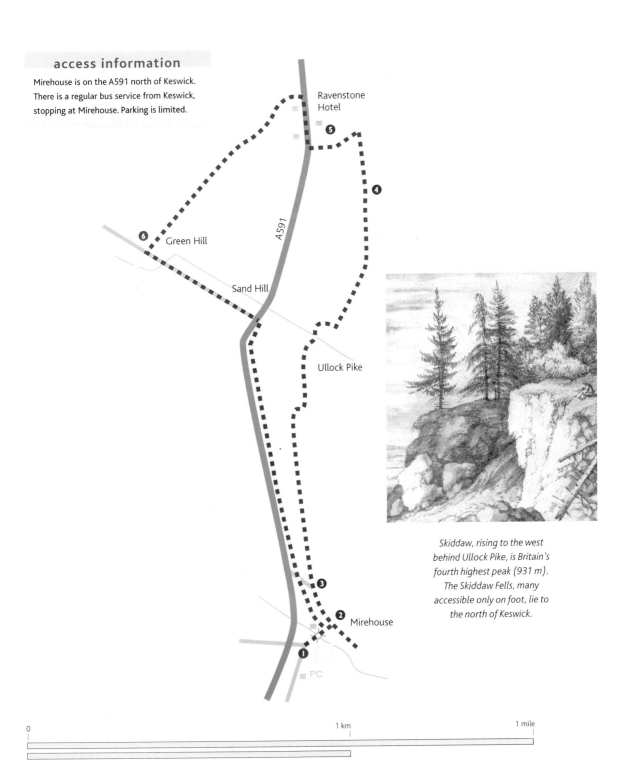

Ravenstone
Hotel

5

4

A591

6
Green Hill

Sand Hill

Ullock Pike

3

2
Mirehouse

1

PC

Skiddaw, rising to the west behind Ullock Pike, is Britain's fourth highest peak (931 m). The Skiddaw Fells, many accessible only on foot, lie to the north of Keswick.

0   1 km   1 mile

▲ Map: Explorer OL 6 & 7
▲ Distance: 10 km/6¼ miles
▲ Walk ID: 341 Jude Howat

Difficulty rating

Time

▲ River, Pub, Wildlife, Great Views

Dungeon Ghyll from Elterwater

This scenic low-level walk follows the course of the Langdale Beck up to Dungeon Ghyll, then returns part way up the side of the valley through some forestry to Elterwater.

1 From the car park, turn left and cross the bridge to the start of the walk. After crossing the bridge, take the road to the right at the T-junction. Follow the track until you reach a mine entrance in the rock face. Opposite this is a footpath heading down the hill towards the beck. Take this path and follow it over a footbridge.

2 You will come out into a car park in the village of Chapel Stile. Walk along the road for around 100 m and take the next footpath to the left. Follow this up a small hill. Continue straight on, keeping on the path just to the right of the white buildings.

3 Keep left. Soon you will cross a bridge over the beck. The path bends to the right. Continue along the track close to the water's edge. Cross the beck again at the bridge. Follow the path up to the main road.

4 Pass through the swing gate and turn left. Walk along the road for around 100 m, then turn left on to the track. Follow it until you rejoin the main road. Turn left and walk along it for 200 m.

5 Turn left on to the track over the bridge. Cross the field towards a farm house. Keep left. Pass through the swing gate, then cross the small bridge and turn left on to the path. Turn right by the disused barn. Follow the path over the hill, heading eastwards.

6 Continue straight on, following the main path all the way until you reach a road. Turn left and follow the road. Turn left again. This road will take you back down to the starting point by the bridge.

access information

Elterwater is on the B5343 to the north west of Ambleside close to the lovely valley of Langdale. There is pay-and-display parking in Elterwater, where this walk starts, but you can also start in Dungeon Ghyll where there is also pay-and-display parking available.

The last section of this track follows a hard track, bordered by woodland, back to the starting point at Elterwater.

▲ Map: Explorer OL 7
▲ Distance: 6 km/3¾ miles
▲ Walk ID: 1390 Jim Grindle

Difficulty rating

Time

▲ Hills or Fells, River, Lake/Loch, Toilets, Museum, Church, National Trust/NTS, Wildlife, Flowers, Great Views, Food Shop, Tea Shop

Alcock Tarn from Grasmere

In this walk a lane gives way to a track rising gradually above the Vale of Grasmere. The tarn itself is an attractive, quiet spot. The return is across beautiful meadows.

1 Turn right as you leave the Information Centre and walk up to the junction by the church. Turn right and go past the main car park to the junction with the main road. Turn left to the new crossing point. Go over and turn right. A lane branches off from the main road. Follow signs for Dove Cottage.

2 Take the left fork along the lane. At the top the lane forks again. Take the left fork and then watch for a track on the left signposted to Alcock Tarn. Where the track splits you will see a little gate.

3 Go through the gate on to the track that leads up to the tarn. Go left of the tarn to a stile in the wall at the far end. Beyond the wall the track leads down to a beck. Cross the bridge and go through the gate on to a drive. This drops to a junction with a lane.

4 Turn left to come to another lane on the left. Turn and follow the lane down to the main road. Just to the right on the main road is a crossing point. Go over and turn left to reach a gate 50 m away.

5 Go along the enclosed track into the field at the end and then follow the right field edge to the first of a sequence of gates. You will reach a newly built bridge. Cross the bridge and turn left.

6 This path will bring you out at the church in the centre of the village. Turn left and take the first turning on the right for the Information Centre.

access information

Grasmere is north of Ambleside on the A591 Ambleside/Keswick road. There are three large car parks in the village and some smaller ones. Buses from Ambleside to Keswick call in at the village.

A picturesque bridge across a lakeland beck is a good place to admire the views after visiting Alcock Tarn.

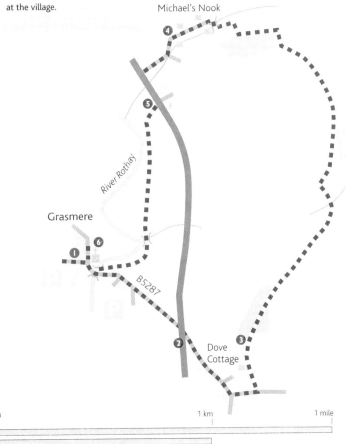

▲ Map: Explorer OL 7
▲ Distance: 8 km/5 miles
▲ Walk ID: 1340 Gary Gray

Difficulty rating

Time

▲ Pub, Toilets, National Trust/NTS, Wildlife, Great Views, Cafe, Food Shop, Good for Kids, Public Transport, Nature Trail, Tea Shop, Woodland

Latterbarrow from Hawkshead

A walk across open fields is followed by a short climb to the summit of Latterbarrow with its tall cairn visible from Hawkshead. The stroll back is through pleasant forest.

❶ Starting from the Red Lion Pub in Hawkshead village, follow the path that runs down the side of the pub to the main road. Go across the road and down another path. The path dog-legs right and then left, and eventually leads to a small footbridge.

❷ Turn left and walk alongside the fence to the corner of the field. Turn right and walk to the far corner where there is a kissing gate. Go through the gate and walk diagonally right across the field. Go through another kissing gate and turn left. There is a signpost for Loanthwaite. The path goes through two further fields and over two stiles. After the second stile follow the path right across the field up to a gate.

❸ Go through the gate and left on to a track towards a large oak tree, which is on the right side of the track. Go over the stile next to the tree and follow the path. There is a fence on your right. Go through the gate and continue on the path, with the fence now on your left side.

The village of Hawkshead is surrounded by fantastic views, not least the summit of Latterbarrow which looms over the town.

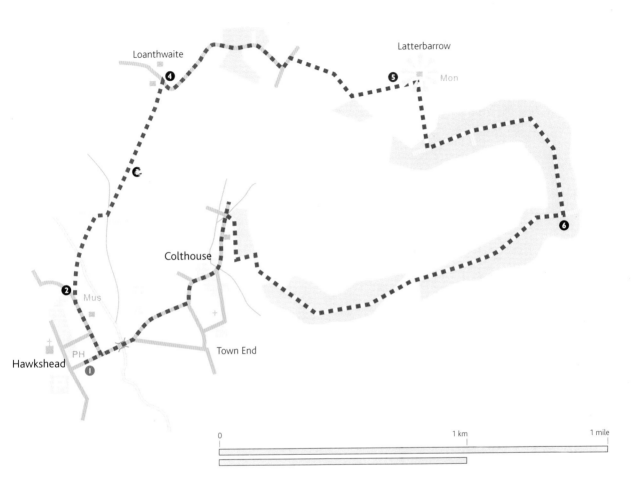

4 The path leads to the right of a farm. At the minor road (Loanthwaite Lane) turn right and follow it to a T-junction. Turn left on to this road and walk on for a short distance. On the right side of the road is a gate signposted Latterbarrow. Go through the gate and follow the track up through the trees. Follow the stone wall to your right and a grassy track to the left leads to the summit.

5 On reaching the summit, you will find the monument and good views. At the monument, go right. The grassy path leads you downhill to a corner and a stone wall and stile. Go left over the stile and follow the path into the forest. The path goes down a steep embankment. Keep to the well-defined main path.

6 The path reaches a gate in a wall, by a T-junction. Go through the gate on to a hard track and follow the signs for Hawkshead. The path leads to a road. Go left and follow the road towards Town End. Turn right at the T-junction and walk along the minor road back to the start at Hawkshead.

access information

The walk starts in Hawkshead, on the B5285 south of Ambleside. There are several large car parks, which are pay-and-display. These get busy at peak holiday times.

Index

acknowledgements

The publishers wish to thank the
following for the use of pictures:
COLLECTIONS: p.50 Sam Walsh
CORBIS: p.8 John Heseltine, 9 Eye
Ubiquitous, 10/11 John Heseltine,
12 Eric Crichton, 15 John Noble,
17 John Heseltine, 18 Derek
Croucher, 22 Richard Klune,
26 + 30 Jon Sparks, 33 Andrew
Brown/Ecoscene, 34/5 Patrick Ward,
38 Eric Crichton, 40 Johnn Heseltine,
43 Alan Towse/Ecoscene, 48 Adam
Woolfitt, 52/3 Michael Busselle,
55 Wildcountry, 58 Andrew
Milliken/Cordaiy Photo Library,
63 Michael Busselle
GETTY IMAGES: p.22 Walter Bibikov
JIM GRINDLE: p.5, 14, 24, 36, 46, 47,
49, 57T, 62
JOYCE AND DOUG HOWAT: p.61
**HUTCHISON PICTURE
LIBRARY:** p.20/1 Bernard Gerard
WILLIAM KEMBERY: p51